The Christian Youth

Written by

C. A. Brewer
Donald Bryan
R. M. Davis
Sharon Davis
Darrell Johns
Anne Wilkins

This book is designed for personal or group study.

PENTECOSTAL PUBLISHING HOUSE
8855 DUNN ROAD
HAZELWOOD, MO 63042-2299

Word Aflame Elective Series

Family Life Selections

The Christian Youth
The Christian Woman
The Christian Man
The Christian Parent

Other Elective Series Volumes

WHY? A Study of Christian Standards
Spiritual Growth and Maturity
Bible Doctrines–Foundation of the Church
Salvation–Key to Eternal Life
The Bible–It's Origin and Use
Strategy for Life for Singles and Young Adults
Spiritual Leadership/Successful Soulwinning
Your New Life
Friendship, Courtship, and Marriage
Purpose at Sunset
Values That Last
Meet the United Pentecostal Church International
Facing the Issues
The Holy Spirit
Life's Choices

EDITORIAL STAFF

R. M. Davis .... Editor
P. D. Buford .... Associate Editor

J. L. Hall .... Editor in Chief
United Pentecostal Church International

©1998 by the Pentecostal Publishing House, Hazelwood, Missouri. All rights reserved.
Reprint History: 1991, 1995, 1998
ISBN 1-56722-034-7

CURRICULUM COMMITTEE: James E. Boatman, P. D. Buford, Dan Butler, R. M. Davis, J. L. Hall, G. W. Hassebrock, Garth E. Hatheway, E. E. Jolley, Chester L. Mitchell, Ronald Nation, Vernon McGarvey, David L. Reynolds, Charles A. Rutter, R. L. Wyser.

Foreword

JERRY JONES
General Secretary
United Pentecostal Church, Int.

All of life can be divided into two parts: becoming and being what we have become. Another way of saying it is that we spend part of our lives learning and preparing and the rest of our lives using what we have learned and being what we have prepared to be. The preparation is usually that part of life that we call youth. Of course, the distinctions are not easily drawn: the challenge is never to stop learning, but while we *are*, to also be always *becoming*. (Some people are always young whatever their age because they never tire of growing.)

The Christian Youth is primarily for young people. It is geared for your problems and challenges. It is mostly, though, about becoming. The first five lessons are for gatherers, those who want to fill their lives with traits that they can draw from over and over: commitment, consecration, purpose, decisiveness, morality, study—the most valuable collection of tools that could be assembled. The last eight lessons are markers on the road. They show us how to take the tools and move toward the goal of service in God's kingdom.

The best thing about *The Christian Youth* is that it is not theory—dry, lifeless opinion handed to us like a vitamin pill just be be swallowed, not enjoyed. Instead, there are people—in every lesson—real, live people struggling, failing, learning, *becoming*. Mirrored in these real people we can see ourselves. We can identify with them, their struggles and their problems. Because of this, these lessons really live.

I know young people will be blessed and challenged by this excellent book. I also have a strong feeling that all of us who are still becoming will be helped by it.

I appreciate Word Aflame for bringing us *The Christian Youth*.

Contents

Chapter	Page
Foreword	3
1. Youth and Commitment	7
2. Youth and Purpose	19
3. Youth and Choices	32
4. Youth and Morality	44
5. Youth and Study	56
6. Youth and Submission	67
7. Youth and Witnessing	80
8. Youth and Worship	92
9. Youth and Availability	103
10. Youth and Expendability	115
11. Youth and Dependability	126
12. Youth and Cooperation	138
13. Youth and Individuality	150

Youth and Commitment

Commit thy way unto the LORD; trust also in him; and he shall bring it to pass.

Psalm 37:5

Start With the Scriptures

Proverbs 3:6
Proverbs 16:3
Mark 8:34-38

Romans 12:1-2
I Timothy 6:20
II Timothy 1:12

Jonathan Edwards, an eighteenth century theologian and preacher, is considered by many to be one of the keenest minds in the history of American religion. From his pulpit went forth a revival, the first Great Awakening that spread through all the American colonies and stirred the hearts of many in Britain as well. As Edwards traveled through the colonies on horseback, entire towns were set ablaze with the fires of revival, and hundreds were converted.

What was the secret of Edwards' anointed life and preaching? Undoubtedly, among other things, it was a wholehearted commitment to God. He voiced that commitment in these words: "Resolved: To follow God with all my heart. Resolved also: Whether others do or not, I will."

Most young people sincerely want their lives to count. They too desire to impact their world for Jesus Christ. And they can. Someone aptly stated that there is no limit to what God can do through a person who is totally committed to Him.

What Is Commitment?

The noun *commitment* is never used in the Scriptures, but *commit,* a verb, is used several times. It means "to deliver a person or thing into the charge or keeping of another." Synonyms of commit include pledge, bind, entrust, choose, consign, and decide.

Commitment implies "no way out" and "no retreat." The committed person "burns his bridges" and "does not look back." After all, Jesus said, "No man, having put his hand to the plough, and looking back, is fit for the kingdom of God" (Luke 9:62).

Jerry White, in his book *The Power of Commitment,* breaks down commitment into three categories. First, there are things which God commits to us, and we in turn practice good stewardship over them. For example, the Apostle Paul wrote to his son in the faith, "O Timothy, keep that which is committed to thy trust, avoiding profane and vain babblings, and oppositions of science falsely so called" (I Timothy 6:20).

Secondly, we commit something to God, and He responds to our confidence in Him. Among other things, we can safely commit our very souls to His care (I Peter 4:19). And because God is trustworthy, with the Apostle Paul we can boldly proclaim, "For

I know whom I have believed, and am persuaded that He is able to keep that which I have committed unto him against that day" (II Timothy 1:12).

Thirdly, we commit ourselves to engage in or refrain from something. We decide, and the Holy Ghost gives us the power to follow through on our commitments. For example, the Apostle Paul, like a dedicated athlete, was committed to living temperately and disciplining his body lest he "should become unfit—not stand the test and be unapproved—and rejected [as a counterfeit]" (I Corinthians 9:25-27, *The Amplified Bible*). God, in turn, empowered him to live a sanctified life.

Components of Commitment

In youth camps and special services, scores of youth commit themselves to God—sometimes over and over—only to discover that after the emotional high has faded so have their commitments. While we cannot discount the role of emotions in commitment, making a commitment should not be solely an emotional experience. Jesus reminded the multitude in a parable "to count the cost" before making a commitment (Luke 14:28).

In his aforementioned book, Jerry White observed that commitment involves the total person: mind, heart and will. To ignore any one of these in the commitment process will eventually result in broken commitments.

The mind. The mind processes information and analyzes truth. It makes decisions. It can even love. Jesus reminded the Pharisees that the first and greatest commandment is to "love the Lord thy God with all thy heart, and with all thy soul, and with all thy mind" (Matthew 22:37).

Psychologists say that 10,000 thoughts pass through the human mind in one day. Little wonder that the strength of our commitment hinges on our thought-life! For steel-strength commitment, we must set our minds on "the higher things" (Colossians 3:2, *The Amplified Bible*).

Youth are sometimes urged to ignore their many doubts and questions. This is dangerous. Commitment demands a fully persuaded mind. The Apostle Paul staunchly declared that he was "persuaded" that nothing could separate him from God's love (Romans 8:38-39). And Abraham, father of the faithful, was "fully persuaded" that God would perform what He promised (Romans 4:21).

The heart. Verbal and mental assent to the lordship of Jesus Christ is not enough. Jesus rebuked the scribes and Pharisees with stinging words: "Ye hypocrites, well did Esaias prophesy of you, saying, This people draweth nigh unto me with their mouth, and honoureth me with their lips; but their heart is far from me" (Matthew 15:7-8).

We must not ignore the heart "for out of it are the issues of life" (Proverbs 4:23). Reverend S. W. Chambers, in a Bible college chapel message, warned the students, "Don't let your mind outgrow your heart!" Why? Lopsided commitments eventually crumble.

Mere knowledge of the Scriptures—even belief in them—will not save anyone. The Apostle Paul reminded the Romans that "with the heart man believeth unto righteousness" (Romans 10:10). And Solomon advised, "Trust in the LORD with all thine heart; and lean not unto thine own understanding" (Proverbs 3:5).

Genuine commitment reaches into the innermost being—to the "real you." It touches the emotions, affections, and desires. It says, "I will give you all!"

The will. Knowing what is right and being stirred emotionally, however, is not enough. We must consciously choose to do right and subordinate our wills to His.

Right doctrine and ecstatic emotional experiences do not justify wrongdoings. James reminded the believers that "to him that knoweth to do good, and doeth it not, to him it is sin" (James 4:17). And Jesus warned, "Not every one that saith unto me, Lord, Lord, shall enter into the kingdom of heaven; but he that doeth the will of my Father which is in heaven" (Matthew 7:21).

Yet it is not enough just to do right. We must do right for the right reasons. In II Chronicles 25:2 we read about a young king who "did that which was right in the sight of the LORD, but not with a perfect heart." Doing "the will of God from the heart," however, is what God expects (Ephesians 6:6).

The goal then of every committed Christian is to do the will of God with a made-up mind and a pure heart!

Biblical Examples of Commitment

Elisha. Elisha was a young farmer when God sent Elijah to anoint him to be a prophet. He was one of the 7,000 in Israel who had not bowed to Baal. Even when Elijah subsequently attempted to stop Elisha from following him, his spiritual desire prevailed.

Elisha burned his plow and killed his oxen. There was no going back. He would follow Elijah and never again return to farming. He was committed to being Elisha's valet until God had other plans for him.

Elisha's commitment to the call of God on his life and to the desire for greater spiritual power paid off. Because he witnessed the catching away of Elijah, he was granted his heart's desire, a double portion of Elijah's spirit. Thus began his own ministry filled with the mighty power of God.

Today God expects no less of a commitment from us. Jesus reminded His followers that love for Him must exceed love for relatives. His language was strong. He said, "If any one comes to Me and does not hate his [own] father and mother [that is, in the sense of indifference for them in comparison with his attitude toward God] and [likewise] his wife and children and brothers and sisters, [yes] and even his own life also, he cannot be My disciple" (Luke 14:26, *The Amplified Bible*).

Job. One day Job was the richest man in the east, the next day one of the very poorest. Calamity struck his household with a vengeance, and he lost his livestock, his servants—with the exception of one—and his children. His reaction to personal tragedy was remarkable. He simply "fell down upon the ground, and worshipped" (Job 1:20).

Before long, Job lost his health. The neighborhood children taunted him, his friends harshly judged him and even the drunkards made him the subject of their songs. Yet with deep conviction he affirmed, "For I know that my redeemer liveth, and that he shall stand at the latter day upon the earth: And though after my skin worms destroy this body, yet in my flesh shall I see God" (Job 19:25-26).

No doubt about it! Job was committed in every sense of the word. He was committed to God regardless of what happened to him, his family, or his possessions. He was committed to the promises of God, and he was committed to the hope of a resurrection.

In the end, though Job never learned what all had transpired behind the scenes, he earned God's stamp of approval on his life. In fact, the Lord rewarded him with twice as much as he had before (Job 42:10).

We can rest assured that our own commitment to God will be tested. It may not be in the same measure as Job's testing, but exam time will come. It is in the hour of testing that the depth of our commitment is proven. It would be good that like Job we could say, "When he hath tried me, I shall come forth as gold" (Job 23:10).

Areas of Commitment

People make commitments all the time—often to the wrong things. Some pursue pleasure, possessions, and popularity. Others commit themselves to unwholesome relationships. Even sincere young people can commit themselves to a hobby, sports, and even education in such a way that spiritual commitments become secondary. With so many demands on their time, talents, and energies, young people should make sure that any commitments they make are rooted firmly in biblical principles.

Committed to a personal relationship with the Lord Jesus Christ. Above all else, we must be committed to the Lord Jesus Christ Himself. To get to know Him, we must spend time every day in prayer and in the reading of His Word. And if we truly love Him, we will deny ourselves, take up our cross and follow Him (Mark 8:34).

Committed to the will of God. Someone once prayed, "Dear God, Your will, nothing more, nothing less, nothing else. Amen." So should our sincere prayer be. We must be committed to doing the will of God whatever it is and wherever it takes us.

Committed to moral purity. Charles Swindoll, in his book *Strengthening Your Grip* observed that "there is a boldness, an unblushing brashness in today's immorality that none can deny. And all of this assaults the senses with such relentless regularity that we need the power of God to walk in purity." It takes commitment to remain virtuous. But after all, it is our "reasonable service" (Romans 12:1).

Committed to the church. We should ask ourselves from time to time, "What would my church be like if everyone were as committed as I?" Commitment to a local body of believers is scriptural. The writer of Hebrews admonished us to forsake not the "assembling of ourselves together" (Hebrews 10:25). We need to be responsible members of our local church body. The church needs dedicated participants, not critical spectators or troublemakers.

Committed to sound doctrine. A young seminarian, days away from graduation, was heard to say, "There is nothing I can absolutely affirm." It should not surprise us that an anything-you-want-to-believe-is-all-right theology has permeated Christendom. Paul forewarned that the day would come when men would not endure sound doctrine (II Timothy 4:3). While others are compromising fundamental doctrines, the church is depending on the leaders of tomorrow to earnestly contend for the one-God, apostolic message.

Committed to holiness. The writer of Hebrews reminded the saints that without holiness no man will see the Lord (Hebrews 12:14). The carnally minded often despise holiness standards, but the consecrated child of God knows that holiness is beautiful (Psalm 96:9). The church rejoices when young men and women are not ashamed to proclaim that "holiness is still in style."

Committed to winning the lost. The Apostle Paul said that God "hath committed unto us the word of reconciliation" (II Corinthians 5:19). In other words, God has entrusted to us the message of salvation to share with a lost world. Because young people often relate best to their peers, a young person committed to evangelism can be a mighty force for Jesus Christ in his school and on the job.

Enemies of Commitment

Apathy. Charles Swindoll, in his book mentioned

earlier, observed that the slogan of the 1940s, "Remember Pearl Harbor!" and the 1960s, "We Shall Overcome!" has each eroded into today's new slogan, "Who Really Cares!" He goes on to note that the tide of apathy in our society has risen.

Tragically, apathy has filtered into the hearts of many Christians. Like never before the church needs young people who care! It needs young men and women who are concerned enough about living right and winning the lost to do something about it.

Committed people are not apathetic. Someone observed that committed people are fighters. Committed health care workers fight disease. Committed law enforcement officials fight crime. Committed educators fight ignorance. And committed soldiers fight for principles.

We can be sure that we will not be transported to heaven on a bed of ease. It will take a fight against sin and Satan. And only committed people wage war. The Apostle Paul said to Timothy, "This charge I commit unto thee. . .war a good warfare" (I Timothy 1:18).

Peer Pressure. The squeeze is on! We can rest confident that when we stand for what is right in this wicked world others will notice and oftentimes attempt to make us conform. Young people are sometimes even pressured by the authority figures in their lives—parents, teachers, employers, and even religious leaders—to succumb to ungodly practices. But we must be careful not to allow even other professing Christians to cause us to act against scriptural principles or to compromise our God-given convictions.

To effectively withstand negative peer pressure, we must have our minds made up well before the pressure is applied. And then with a right attitude, we must inform those who pressure us that we will not yield to unrighteousness—not then or ever. It would help to be "ready always to give an answer to every man that asketh you a reason of the hope that is in you with meekness and fear" (I Peter 3:15).

But peer pressure is not just a modern-day scourge. Timothy faced it as a young man. The Apostle Paul wrote in his letter to the Romans, "Don't let the world around you squeeze you into its own mold, but let God re-mold your minds from within, so that you may prove in practice that the plan of God for you is good, meets all his demands and moves toward the goal of true maturity" (Romans 12:2, *Phillips*).

Fear. Jerry White, in his book alluded to previously, stated that "fear of commitment is epidemic in the Western world." Some fear the responsibility commitment brings. Others are afraid to sell out completely to God for fear that He has ulterior designs on their lives. They worry that if they said an unreserved yes, God would ship them off to the bush country of Africa—single, at that.

However, "the will of God," as someone so aptly said, "will not lead us where the grace of God cannot keep us." Someone else reminded us, "Out of the will of God there is no such thing as success; in the will of God there cannot be failure."

We can overcome our fear of commitment by committing ourselves in small things and then in increasingly greater things as we mature. And as we commit ourselves, we will discover that God will enable us to keep our commitments.

Benefits of Commitment

When we commit our lives unreservedly to the Lord Jesus Christ, we can expect to enjoy the abundant life. The Scriptures are replete with precious promises to those who would dare say an unequivocal yes to Him.

God will give us the desires of our hearts. David said, "Commit thy way unto the LORD; trust also in him; and he shall bring it to pass" (Psalm 37:5). Bring what to pass? The preceding verse gives us the answer: the desires of our hearts. When our total lifestyle pleases God, He delights to give us the things we desire and to answer our secret petitions.

God will direct our paths. Someone called ours the "aimless society." Yet the Lord promised to direct those who commit their ways to Him (Proverbs 3:6). It is especially vital that proper commitments be made in one's youth. Such commitments often chart the course of a person's life.

God will bring stability into our lives. The single-mindedness of a committed person brings stability into his life. On the contrary, James said, "A double minded man is unstable in all his ways" (James 1:8). When we commit our works to the Lord, we have the promise that He will cause our thoughts to become agreeable to His will and that our plans will be established and succeed (Proverbs 16:3, *The Amplified Bible*).

God will give us eternal rewards. When we respond responsibly to the things God has committed to us—our talents, our finances, our bodies, the gospel—rewards will come. Like the faithful steward, we will someday hear those words, "Well done, good and faithful servant; thou hast been faithful over a few things, I will make thee ruler over many things: enter thou into the joy of thy lord" (Matthew 25:23).

Yes, commitment is costly. But the power and joy of a committed life and the rewards to come make it well worth any price!

Test Your Knowledge

1. What does *commit* mean?

2. List several synonyms of the word *commit*.

3. What are the three basic types of commitment?

4. We must commit what three aspects of ourselves to God?

5. In what areas did Elisha commit himself?

6. In what areas did Job commit himself?

7. What are some wrong commitments youth sometimes make?

8. List several areas in which we can commit ourselves.

9. List three enemies of commitment.

10. List several benefits of committing our lives to God.

Apply Your Knowledge

Jonathan Edwards penned a series of personal commitments that still inspire us today. One such statement reads: "Resolved, never to do anything which I should be afraid to do if it were the last hour of my life." Another one of his commitments was alluded to earlier in the chapter.

Prayerfully consider what commitments God would like you personally to make to Him. Jot down your thoughts in this form: "Resolved. . . ."

Expand Your Knowledge

Choose a biography or an autobiography of one of our Pentecostal pioneers and seek to discover areas in which they made personal commitments to the Lord Jesus Christ.

The Pentecostal Publishing House carries a wide selection of such books, which may be ordered from its catalog.

Youth and Purpose 2

For the Lord GOD will help me; therefore shall I not be confounded: therefore have I set my face like a flint, and I know that I shall not be ashamed.
Isaiah 50:7

Start With the Scriptures

Proverbs 20:18
Daniel 1-12
Acts 2:42; 11:22-23

Ephesians 3:11
II Timothy 3:10
James 1:1-12

The girl came running blindly from around the back of the school, clumsily running into other students and finally tripping over one which sent her sprawling on her hands and knees. Her long hair was in total disarray, many strands cemented to her face by the streaming torrents of tears raging down her cheeks. As she looked up with desperation, her incoherent heavings of emotion changed into wailing pleas for help.

"Help, please....Won't somebody help!" she

screamed. "It's John. . . .He's dying."

Between the sobbing and the screaming those who had gathered around Cindy were able to piece together the source of her distress. Her boyfriend had slashed his wrists and was bleeding to death at the back of the school property.

While some scurried off to help John and others ran to alert school officials and secure medical help, a few remained to comfort Cindy. The few words that Cindy spoke were like darts of acid in their hearts.

"He was hurting so badly. He seemed so unsure of himself. He just refused to go on. He said, 'Life has no meaning, no purpose. . . .It's useless to live.'"

This story is a frightfully realistic scenario among teens and young adults today. Pressures are intense and competition is keen. It seems that problems loom larger than they ever have, but it also seems there is so little time to deal with them. This is a furiously fast-paced world. If ever a person has needed a sure sense of purpose in life, it is now.

Of the many characteristics a person may possess, perhaps the most important is that of purpose. A person without purpose struggles all of his life, never quite sure where he fits into society and practically always frustrated with himself. Yet a person with a strong sense of national and personal purpose is filled with self-assurance and confidence. He knows not only what his purpose in life is, but also how he will endeavor to achieve that purpose.

The modern suicide rate, especially among youth, is staggering. A healthy person who is comfortable with himself can hardly understand why someone would choose to end his life. To the healthy, confident person life is one of his most valuable possessions—priceless to say the least. But to a frustrated, disturbed individual, life is meaningless and can easily be discarded in a weak moment. Possibly the primary difference between such contrasting individuals is a strong purpose in life.

Whether we understand the awful problem of teen suicide or not, we certainly should realize its fact. It is a real problem and we should recognize it and deal with it. Rather than dismiss suicide as something that could never affect us or our friends, we should take a positive step toward its prevention. We should first examine our basic sense of purpose in life.

People Need Purpose

Purpose is defined as "an object or result aimed at: intention," or as "resolution, determination." It is the whole direction in which a person governs his life and the total of energy he expends in doing so. Purpose is the "bottom line" of one's life; it is the means and the end of life all in one.

Having purpose in life is a scriptural admonition. God set the example of purpose for us in all of His divine actions. Everything He accomplished was for specific purposes in the present time and for an ultimate purpose, which He has revealed to us through His Word, in eternity. Several facts are known about God's many purposes and His ultimate purpose.
- They are on behalf of humanity (Ephesians 1:11).
- They will cause Satan's final destruction (I John 3:8).
- They are absolute (Jeremiah 4:28; 51:29; Isaiah 14:24-27; 46:11).
- They are eternal (Ephesians 3:11).

Mankind is on earth by no ability or goodness of his own, but by the purpose of God. Every aspect of the Creation was designed to complement its apex—the creation of man in the image of God. Man was made for the pleasure and worship of God that in everything he should glorify the Lord.

Because man is made by the Lord and for Him, he can only be happy when his purpose in life is in harmony with that of God. Only in his total devotion and dedication to God can a man know complete human fulfillment. For this reason the happiest people on earth are not only individuals of great purpose, but they are ones whose purpose is anchored securely in Jesus Christ.

People with Purpose

Many great Bible characters recorded in both Old and New Testaments displayed a strong sense of purpose. Noah exhibited his purpose by spending more than a hundred years building the ark at the commandment of God. He evidently suffered scorn and ridicule by many people as he obeyed God in an unusual fashion. Had he been selfish and arrogant he would not have committed his life to the plan of God, but because he obeyed, he saved his family from destruction.

Abraham was a man of great purpose. God called him and presented him with a tremendous challenge—leave his relatives and country to sojourn to a land with which he was completely unfamiliar. Abraham made his share of mistakes, but he obeyed God and that is what counts most in life.

Nehemiah's sense of purpose made possible the rebuilding of the walls of Jerusalem (Nehemiah 2:1-5). He brought direction to the nation of Judah after its return to Jerusalem from captivity in Babylon. Upon hearing of the desolate condition of Jerusalem, Nehemiah was consumed of a tremendous burden to champion its rebuilding. This he did in a phenomenal fashion, seeing the walls rebuilt in only fifty-two days. The Book of Nehemiah is a beautiful study in the subject of godly purpose.

The Apostle Paul is one from the New Testament who exhibited great purpose. Prior to his conversion to Christianity he maintained a tremendous sense of purpose toward the cause of Judaism. After his conversion Paul directed his zeal and purpose toward spreading the gospel of Jesus Christ and establishing new churches. His total commitment and selfless sacrifice left behind him a legacy of accomplishment, all because of a keen sense of divine purpose.

Paul's realization of his life-purpose is readily observable throughout his writings, but perhaps is no clearer than as recorded in Acts 21:13: "I am ready not to be bound only, but also to die at Jerusalem for the name of the Lord Jesus." One's purpose should not only be a cause for which he is willing to live his life, but one as well for which he is willing to die.

Die is exactly what the King of purpose did for the cause of the salvation of mankind. Jesus Christ was born, lived, died and was resurrected for the ultimate purpose of man's redemption. His is the greatest illustration of devotion to a purpose.

There are so many others throughout the Bible who displayed valiant spirits of dedication to the cause and purpose of life. In the Book of Daniel are depicted four young individuals who demonstrated a strong sense of purpose. Their lives reflected many characteristics of Christianity which were products of their commitment to a firm life-purpose devoted to God.

Products of Purpose

Daniel was only a teenager when taken into Babylonian captivity to serve in the king's court. He was probably about sixteen. His three companions,

Hananiah, Mishael, and Azariah (unfortunately, known by their pagan, Babylonian names: Shadrach, Meshach, and Abednego) were probably all about the same age as Daniel. Yet these teenagers had evidently developed some tremendous qualities of Christian character which were products of their devotion to God. This is revealed through their consistent refusal to compromise their commitment to the Hebrew God, although given numerous opportunities.

These young people were chosen to serve in the king's court and learn the Chaldean language because of their physical and mental qualities, which were certainly to be appreciated. God was much more interested, however, in their spiritual character than in their skills, knowledge, and abilities.

That these young men had a great sense of national and divine purpose is quickly seen in the first chapter of the Book of Daniel. Surfacing as the obvious leader of the four youths, Daniel purposed in his heart that he would not defile himself by eating the king's meat or by drinking his wine (Daniel 1:8). This decision of abstinence was one of self-control and discipline in keeping himself pure from the idolatry of the Babylonians.

In Babylon, the Hebrew God was not honored but was mocked. The people served idols. Even the meat that they ate was a form of worship to their false gods. Daniel realized this and desired to glorify Jehovah in the midst of the Babylonian pagans. This he did by refusing their meat and drink.

Young people need a basic sense of purpose and stedfastness to God and that which is right. Many opportunities come to compromise their knowledge of right and wrong at school, on the job, with certain friends, or even out with the church youth group. When such temptations confront them, only a genuine faithfulness to a deep commitment and resolve can keep them true to what they know God desires of them.

The stedfast purpose of the Hebrew youths caused several prominent Christian characteristics to be recognized in their lives.

These youth possessed a quality of unity (Daniel 2:17-18). In the second year of King Nebuchadnezzar's reign he was troubled with dreams. His spirit was troubled and he could not sleep. Then the king called for the magicians, astrologers and the sorcerers—all of Babylon's wise men—to interpret his dreams. None of the king's wise men, however, could provide an interpretation. This angered the king greatly and he set forth a decree to destroy all of Babylon's wise men.

As the king's men came to slay Daniel and his friends, Daniel sought an audience with the king to request time, that he could receive the interpretation. He went before the king and made his request, and time was given for them to interpret the dreams.

Daniel went immediately to his companions and shared the situation with them. They then sought the mercies of God, all four of them together, that they could receive the interpretation.

Daniel obviously recognized the strength of unity. We can accomplish much more together than any one of us can do alone. There is strength and power in unity. Jesus said, "If two of you shall agree on earth as touching any thing that they shall ask, it shall be done for them of my Father which is in heaven" (Matthew 18:19). Daniel did not attempt to be a "super hero." He sought and obtained the strength of his friends through unity. Their common purpose provided a foundation for unity.

Daniel was sensitive to God's Spirit (Daniel 2:19). After Daniel joined in unity with his friends to seek God's answer, then the secret was revealed to him in a night vision. Such an experience does not just happen; it is the product of an ongoing relationship with God.

Teens should not wait until they are in trouble to seek God. If they nurture a daily relationship with the Lord, they can be sensitive to Him in times of difficulty and can hear from Him.

Daniel was quick to worship God (Daniel 2:19-23). Daniel did not seem to feel smug or confident within himself when he received the interpretation of the dream. He simply began to worship God and glorify Him. He was quick to acknowledge that all wisdom, might and knowledge belong to God. He did not exalt himself or feel proud of his accomplishment. He knew the glory belonged to the Lord.

God moves through the medium of worship. The more teens worship Him, the more He is able to do for them. As they acknowledge Him in their lives, He directs their paths. (See Proverbs 3:5-7.) We can actually worship our way through problems.

Our purpose in life will direct our worship. If our purpose in life is Christ-centered, then our worship will keep Christ central.

Daniel possessed the fine quality of compassion (Daniel 2:24-25). Daniel did not seek to save only his and his friends' lives, but also the lives of his enemies.

When Daniel delivered the secret of the dream unto the king, he could have sought to save only the lives of himself and the three Hebrew children. They could have immediately been elevated in Babylon through the elimination of the others. Some people would delight in the elimination of their enemies. Daniel, however, possessed compassion for his enemies. There was no evil desire in his heart to see them destroyed; therefore, he sought to save all of the wise men's lives.

Compassion for others is a high quality that we all need. Sometimes it is tempting for a teen to be cruel to his peers, not thinking of how he himself would feel in the same situation. If we want mercy for ourselves, however, we must first be merciful to others. (See Proverbs 11:17; Matthew 5:7.)

If God's eternal purpose has become our purpose we will want to help others and lead them to salvation. We will want to live and die for others instead of living selfishly.

Daniel gave the honor and glory to God (Daniel 2:28). He was not seeking glory for himself. He was not interested as much in what men thought of him as he was in what they thought of his God. "There is a God in heaven that revealeth secrets," he said (Daniel 2:28).

God will use teens who are quick to give Him glory. He will not share His glory with another (Isaiah 42:8; 48:11). If we are prone to glorify God and not ourselves, He will readily use us in great ways.

Also seen in the life of young Daniel was a spirit of selflessness and sharing (Daniel 2:47-49). Daniel revealed the full interpretation of the dream to Nebuchadnezzar and gave all the credit and glory to God. Nebuchadnezzar responded by acknowledging Daniel's God as a God of gods and a Lord of kings (Daniel 2:47).

Nebuchadnezzar immediately elevated Daniel to ruler over the whole province of Babylon and graced him with many gifts. Daniel, however, could not accept such honor and forget his friends who had sought God with him for the answer. He remembered Hananiah, Mishael and Azariah by requesting a place of leadership for them also. How easy it would have been for Daniel to forget his friends in the time of honor. But his deep sense of character would not permit him to overlook their sacrifice and assistance in prayer and unity.

It is easy to seek the help of our peers when we

are in trouble but forget them when things are going well. A friend is a friend in the good times as well as the bad times. A real friend loveth at all times (Proverbs 17:17).

Daniel and his friends all exhibited the qualities of faithfulness and fearlessness when tempted (Daniel 3:16-18; 6:10). It was probably about fifteen to twenty years later that Nebuchadnezzar made a new golden image, an idol, and commanded all to fall down before it and worship it at the sounding of the music. The three Hebrews refused to bow and worship the idol and were called into question before the king. They boldly answered him, "We are not careful to answer thee in this matter. If it be so, our God whom we serve is able to deliver us. . . .But if not, be it known unto thee, O king, that we will not serve thy gods, nor worship the golden image which thou hast set up" (Daniel 3:16-18).

With the same boldness and courage Daniel faced the conflict of the lions' den when he stedfastly prayed in violation of a new law. His purpose supplied him with true courage.

There was a basic quality of courage and faithfulness that caused them to lay their lives "on the line." They knew what was right and were determined to do it even if it cost them their lives.

Sometimes the cost of living for God in front of peers looks tremendously enormous to a teen. The challenge to compromise his knowledge of truth is ever before him. Yet he has a promise that if he is faithful to God, God will be faithful to him.

They exhibited prayerfulness (Daniel 6:10). This was especially obvious in Daniel's life. Jealousy caused certain renegades to conspire against Daniel, which they did by having the king outlaw prayer for thirty days. They knew Daniel would not discontinue his prayer—not even for a brief season.

They were right; Daniel prayed as always. Daniel

did not decide to break the decree. There was no decision to make; he simply continued to pray as he always did—three times each day.

Because of his established purpose of heart, Daniel faced the lions' den bravely. He had a supreme trust in God and the Lord did not disappoint him; God shut the mouths of the lions and Daniel was delivered.

God blesses those who are consistent and persistent in prayer. Prayer becomes the great shield of God's protection and providence in our lives each day.

Even teenagers need to pray. Prayer is not only for overcoming problems; it builds and maintains a person's relationship with Jesus Christ. It is his relationship with God that gives a person confidence that whatever comes, God will be with him and protect him.

Prayer is the only characteristic that both introduces us to the purpose of God and is a product of that purpose. We pray to find the will of God and to become a part of God's kingdom. Then we continue to pray because we have found genuine purpose in God's kingdom.

Daniel possessed an excellent spirit (Daniel 5:12). He did not think more highly of himself than he should have. (See Romans 12:3.) His attitude was right. This was perhaps Daniel's highest quality of character.

How important is our attitude! Though every other area of a Christian's life may be in order, his attitude can ruin it all. Although men judge others by the obvious, outward signs, God weighs men's spirits (attitudes). (See Proverbs 16:2 and I Samuel 16:7.)

A person's attitude is so important that he will probably only possess the other qualities of Christian character if his attitude is first right. As a man thinks in his heart, so is he (Proverbs 23:7). We are only as successful and our life as meaningful as the thoughts we dwell on. The central part of a human being is his thought patterns.

Power of Purpose

Divine purpose and its many accompanying characteristics provide power for our lives. It helps keep us on "track" with our lifetime objectives clearly visible at all times. A person without purpose wanders aimlessly through life, but he who has purpose has goals and he reaches constantly for them. He knows where he is headed.

The ultimate power afforded by divine purpose is that of the redemptive grace of Jesus Christ. It is the impelling, motivating force which will one day take us to our reward in heaven.

Pathway to Purpose

"So how do I obtain true purpose in life?" one may ask.
- Recognize the basic purpose of God.
- Understand the purpose of the church.
- Find a place within God's plan.
- Take action.

God has a place for every one of us and He wants us to be saved. We can know His purpose and we can find our place within that purpose in the church.

When we submit ourselves to God we have taken the first step toward knowing God's purpose for our life. Through obeying the plan of salvation, praying, fasting, reading and memorizing our Bible, attending church, being faithful, and fellowshiping with others, we can find our place and fulfill it. Then with purpose we can strive to obtain the mastery of the crown of life.

Test Your Knowledge

1. Define purpose.
2. Because man is made by the Lord and for Him, he can only be happy when his _____ in life is in _____ with that of God.
3. Prayer is the only characteristic that both introduces us to the _____ of God and is a _____ of that purpose.
4. We are only as successful and our life as meaningful as the _____ we dwell on.
5. The ultimate power afforded by divine purpose is that of the _____ _____ of Jesus Christ.
6. When we _____ ourselves to God we have taken the first step toward knowing God's _____ for our life.

Apply Your Knowledge

Examine your personal life with regard to purpose. What are your goals? Do you have short-term and long-term goals?

Take a piece of paper and write your short-term goals. Then write your long-range goals. Begin this week to take steps toward reaching your goals.

Expand Your Knowledge

Several men are mentioned in the lesson as examples of men with purpose. An indepth study of several of these men will add to your understanding of purpose and its accompanying benefits.

A study of the Books of Daniel and Nehemiah will add to this study, also.

3 Youth and Choices

And if it seem evil unto you to serve the LORD, choose you this day whom ye will serve; whether the gods which your fathers served that were on the other side of the flood, or the gods of the Amorites, in whose land ye dwell: but as for me and my house, we will serve the LORD.

Joshua 24:15

Start With the Scriptures

Genesis 13
I Kings 3
I Kings 9-11
Proverbs 11:14

An Amazing Privilege

Many people can remember when buying ice cream was simply deciding if they wanted vanilla, chocolate, or strawberry. But today a trip to the ice cream store leaves a person bewildered, trying to decide between "Rocky Road," "Peaches 'n Cream" and many other flavors. And these decisions are the simple ones! The broader, more serious issues of careers, marriage partners, lifestyles and eternal salvation leave a mind numb with their complexity and the consequences of improper decisions.

It is not easy to choose, and making choices is sometimes frightening and confusing. But we should never forget for a moment that the option to choose is possibly the greatest single privilege we possess! When God created the universe and our beautiful world, He put everything, with one exception, under His direct control. He controls the stars, the winds, the animals, and all life. The sun and moon follow His bidding, and at His command the tempest-tossed seas become still. What is the one exception? The human will. The *will* is defined as "volition" or simply "the ability to choose."

Consequently, life is a constant array of choices. Through our choices we prove to God how much we love Him and want to serve Him. Marriages, careers, habits, lifestyles, worship—all have to be chosen and our choices reflect the inner man and what we really are. What an opportunity, but what a responsibility! "For unto whomsoever much is given, of him shall be much required" (Luke 12:48).

With man's inventiveness, life has produced many options. But one thing is certain; we cannot live every kind of lifestyle, every kind of philosophy, every kind of option available. We must choose. And we do need help to know what is right to choose. How do we know what is right? How do we choose?

The Standard for Wise Choices

Almost all of life's choices have one of two consequences. A choice brings either reward or punishment. Just as fire can burn us or cook our food, or as water can sustain us or drown us, so can choices bring growth or failure.

Making choices without a standard is like shooting an arrow without a target. The rightness or wrongness of the choice can only be judged by its comparison to the standard. We know every good gift and every perfect gift is from above (James 1:17) and "that in me (that is, in my flesh,) dwelleth no good thing" (Romans 7:18). Therefore, the human mind is capable of justifying any kind of behavior, action or decision, no matter how bizarre or unusual!

For instance, we know murder is wrong because God set the standard, "Thou shalt not kill." And without God's direction of "Thou shalt not steal," we could assume that life is a "survival of the fittest," and feel justified in stealing. Without God's concept of marriage and morality, mankind could completely justify adultery and fornication, feeling that "life owed me something." Without the proper foundation, we cannot even take wise advantage of our choices.

So the first step in making wise choices is to realize that we cannot make them without God's help. We must follow the principles He has laid down for us in His Word. Solomon, who was the wisest man in the Bible, realized his need when he asked for wisdom from God to help him make the right choices. (See I Kings 3:5-15.) It was not enough for Solomon to be sitting on the throne, heir to the lineage of David and with a kingdom to rule over. He wanted wisdom from God to help him rule the nation. God answered Solomon's prayer for wisdom, and He will also give us wisdom. "If any of you lack wisdom, let him ask of God, that giveth to all men liberally. . .and it shall be given him" (James 1:5).

"But seek ye first the kingdom of God and his righteousness; and all these things shall be added unto you" (Matthew 6:33).

No decision in life is too small or too large for God. He wants to be involved in our decision making. All wise choices are made by first seeking God.

How to Make a Choice

The importance of choosing well in life cannot be overstated. Much sorrow, depression, guilt and sin in life has resulted from not heeding God's direction and guidance. So how do we make wise choices in life? What are some of the principles we should follow?

Seek wise counsel. "Where no counsel is, the people fall: but in the multitude of counsellors there is safety" (Proverbs 11:14). The principle of seeking counsel is a sound one. Rarely can one person's thinking equal the combined wisdom and thought of several experienced people. It is always wise to seek the advice of mature, stable people, especially one's pastor and parents. Although the final decision will be the individual's to make, counselors can give insight gained from experience. Only a foolish person would try to decide life's most important decisions without counseling with others. Admitting that we do not know it all and seeking counselors who are mature and will give us godly advice is an excellent course to follow.

After Solomon's death in I Kings 11, Rehoboam became king of Israel. At the request of Jeroboam to make the people's financial burden lighter, Rehoboam sought counsel from the old men and the young men. These two groups had opposite advice for Rehoboam, and he chose to forsake the experience of the older men and follow the advice of the young men. His decision was a poor one because the people of Israel promptly rebelled and the nation of Israel became divided. What was Rehoboam's mistake? He listened to poor, unwise counsel.

Take time to decide. Although some choices may require quick decisions, the wise person will always take plenty of time to decide. Strength is promised to those who wait upon the Lord (Isaiah 40:31). Giving ourselves time to decide will allow us to look at all the options and potential problem areas. The more we think our way through a problem, generally the wiser the decision.

Seek the kingdom of God first. God has promised to add to our lives if we will seek His will first. Since choice is an opportunity to surrender our will to God, a wise person will always seek God first. "Seek ye first the kingdom of God, and his righteousness; and all these things shall be added unto you" (Matthew 6:33).

When a person approaches a decision, he should open his mind completely to the will of God. Many people approach God with a preconceived desire and hope He will approve it rather than being willing to do whatever God wants. If a person is truly desirous of the will of God, he will find it in his search. This period of decision making is the most critical because only with the foundation of God's principles undergirding a person's choices can life be lived fully. "Except the LORD build the house, they labor in vain that build it" (Psalm 127:1).

Finding the will of God is easier than most people think. First, any choice which is outside the boundaries of scriptural principles can never be pleasing to God. For example, if a Christian lady is seeking employment at a place which would require her to dress immodestly, she need pray no further. That option is off limits. Just as Adam and Eve had plenty of choices in the Garden of Eden, they also had areas which were forbidden.

Just as Solomon's idolatrous wives led him away from God, so can marrying an unsaved, nonbelieving person lead a Christian away from God because they are unequally yoked together. (See II Corinthians 6:14.) Seeking the kingdom of God first would eliminate the temptation caused by the unsaved person's good looks, financial position, or personality. Desiring any career which would require a person to compromise his Christian principles would be off limits. Although these choices seem easy to make, many young people stumble over them and live their lives outside the will of God. We will do well to put God's principles first!

Use common sense. A person should never fail to use the power of common sense in making a choice. Although a Christian is to walk by faith, God also equips a person with ability and talents to do His will. Therefore, many decisions can be made more easily by considering our own interests, strengths, and weaknesses.

If a young lady has musical ability, she may consider using her talent for a career. If a young man is good in science and math, he could probably pursue an engineering degree and still please the Lord. However, many poor choices are made because the individual did not consider his financial position, his own motivations and talents, and his weaknesses. Many decisions result in trouble because even at the beginning they lacked common sense. We must never ignore this vital element in making choices.

How to Recover From a Wrong Choice

Despite the best efforts put into decision making, we will make some wrong decisions. No one will go through life without having to recover from some bad decisions. What does a person do if he has made a wrong choice?

First we should expect to live through the consequences. When failure comes, whether in a home, career, or finances, it is difficult to keep a proper perspective. Suddenly it seems as if nothing is going right. Satan can so cloud a person's mind with fear and discouragement that the "Elijah syndrome" sweeps across his mind with regularity.

In I Kings 19, Elijah had just faced his greatest challenge and won with the destruction of the false prophets of Baal. But because of the fear tactics of Jezebel, the king of Israel's wife, Elijah fled for his life and ended up discouraged and asking God to take his life. We need not fear, however. The Bible is filled with ordinary people who overcame their difficulties.

Next, we need to admit the wrong decision to ourselves, to God, and perhaps to a trusted friend. It is hard for us to admit we were wrong. The old adage "live and learn" is not true for all people. Many live but never learn. But by looking at the mistake objectively, we can see where we made the mistake and not repeat it.

If there is sin involved in the mistake, we must repent of it before God. Psalm 51 is a beautiful example of David's repentant prayer after he made the grievous mistake with Bathsheba. "If we confess our sins, he is faithful and just to forgive us our sins" (I John 1:9).

Next, we must keep the faith. Once our confidence has been shattered, it is difficult to remember all the right decisions we have made. We soon forget all the times God helped in the past.

In Mark 6, Jesus' disciples witnessed the feeding of the multitude by the miraculous breaking and multiplying of the bread. The disciples rejoiced in the power of God, but then were sent into a storm. They immediately forgot what Jesus had just performed. In the midst of the storm, Jesus came to the disciples and reminded them of the miracle of the bread and the feeding of thousands with His power. But because of the immediate crisis, the disciples quickly forgot the past help they had received from the Lord and consequently became very frightened and unable to decide what to do.

It is hard for one to do wrong when he really wants to do right. Despite the mistakes made, most people make more right decisions than wrong ones.

Next, we must remember God's peace. In John 14:27 Jesus spoke, "Peace I leave with you, my peace I give unto you: not as the world giveth, give I unto you. Let not your heart be troubled, neither let it be afraid." God's peace is not just the cessation of hostilities, but actually the mending of that which is broken. God does not discard fragments but uses all that is given to Him.

Finally, we wait for the salvation of the Lord. God is a God of timing and He never moves off schedule. However, our ways are not His ways and often we get discouraged because we feel God is not going to move. We should have enough confidence in God to wait for Him. He can heal the hurt of painful memories, cause bitterness to leave, and bring joy back to a person. The sun will shine again.

Roadblocks to Making Choices

Choices in life become increasingly important as a person matures. Whereas children are faced with simple questions, a teenager possibly faces the decisions of whom to marry or what career to choose. Adults face the difficulties of raising a family, health, and a myriad of complex issues. Furthermore, as a person ages, the consequences of a wrong decision are greater.

Because many people have made wrong choices, they find themselves afraid and unable to choose. This fear stands as a roadblock to recovery. But making no decision is in itself also a decision and in very few cases can a person simply do nothing. Decisions have to be made.

"There is no fear in love; but perfect love casteth

out fear" (I John 4:18). Perfect love implies perfect trust. Therefore, to displace the fear, we put our trust in the Lord, make the choice, and let God give us the peace of His presence. (See Romans 8:28.)

Procrastination is another roadblock to making choices. Making a correct decision strengthens the heart and gives direction. However, many simply put off a decision and cannot seem to ever become motivated enough to decide.

We can break the chain of procrastination by beginning to do something involving the decision. Perhaps gathering additional information or talking to a friend about the decision to be made will begin the process of choosing. We can make a daily commitment to pray and seek God until the decision is made. Putting our thoughts on paper and listing the advantages and disadvantages of each option will help. This technique will keep our attention focused on the choice until the decision can be made.

Subtle Choices

A person's reputation before men and God is established by the choices he makes. The major decisions, such as marriage, salvation, and career will obviously affect a person's life and reputation in every way. But according to Song of Solomon 2:15, it is the "little foxes that spoil the vines." In reality, daily choices affect a person's major decisions. Who a person associates with, what he finds pleasure in, where he sits in church, and what he wears are all examples of important daily choices. These daily choices ultimately establish one's reputation and pattern of living and provide the basis for the important choices when they are made.

Cemented Choices

People do not usually watch cement harden

because it is too boring. At first the cement is liquid and can be formed in any shape. But once it is poured, it begins a gradual hardening process. At one point a person's initials can be carved into it, but if we wait too long the cement will get too hard. Once it sets, there is no changing it outside of breaking it.

Although a person's choices can be changed, they are much like the cement. As a person progresses in life, the consequences of decisions become more costly. He will finally reach the point described in Revelation 22:11. "He that is unjust, let him be unjust still: and he which is filthy, let him be filthy still: and he that is righteous, let him be righteous still." At some point we cannot change. There will be no more choices.

Solomon's advice in Ecclesiastes 12:1, "Remember now thy Creator in the days of thy youth," is very important for a young person. Solomon recognized the value of choosing wisely while still young, and the best way to do this is to look to God. We must not become cemented into a defiled or lost condition because of the impulses of youth.

Putting It All Together

Genesis chapter thirteen records one of the clearest examples of choosing recorded in the Bible. Both Abraham and Lot needed to make a decision that would profoundly affect their lives because it involved where each would live. Let us look at how they made their decisions. First, we notice the similarity between the men. Both were wealthy. Both were righteous. Both followed God. But when decision time came, the differences between the men became apparent. Abraham offered Lot the opportunity to choose which direction he would go and live.

Lot's first mistake was that he failed to seek the kingdom of God. No record is given that Lot sought the Lord at all. While Abraham built at least seven altars in his lifetime, it is not recorded that Lot built any. His personal relationship to God was evidently flawed, and that affected his decision.

Next, Lot evidently failed to consult with any counselors. His decision was made alone. Furthermore, Lot possibly made a quick decision. The Bible does not indicate that Lot spent any time praying and analyzing the choice before him. His decision, perhaps hastily made, was the plain where the cities of Sodom and Gomorrah were located. He apparently failed to consider the impact these wicked cities could have on his family and himself. His choice to associate with Sodom and Gomorrah caused him to be affected by the judgment of God.

Meanwhile, Abraham had sought God, made the proper decisions, and continued his life as a man of God. Abraham's right relationship with God prepared him to make the right choices, regardless of his environment. Abraham died with honor; Lot died in disgrace. Two choices made by two men provided different destinies.

As we look to the future, we need to remember the amazing privilege of choice. We should choose well and wisely while young. The days of our youth are critical decision times, but God has promised to help us. As we remember Him now, our future will continue to remain bright.

Test Your Knowledge

1. The will of a person is defined as _____
2. Why does God give a human the power to choose? _____
3. What is the first step required in making wise choices? _____

4. Proverbs 11:14 records which principle for making a choice? _____

5. Quick decisions are usually _____ decisions.

6. Seeking the kingdom of God first defines the _____ from which to choose.

7. List the steps which will help a person recover if he makes a bad decision.

_____
_____
_____
_____
_____

8. Two major roadblocks to making choices are _____ and _____.

9. Ecclesiastes 12:1 outlines what advice concerning decisions? _____

10. Why did Lot make such a poor choice concerning his future? _____

Apply Your Knowledge

Make an appointment with the people who influence your life the most and ask them to tell you the major good and bad decisions they have made in life. Their information will greatly benefit you.

Complete a study of the major characters in the Bible who reached decision points in their lives and record in a notebook how they made decisions.

List the major decisions you will be facing in the near future and begin to seek counsel in preparation for making the right choices.

Expand Your Knowledge

Read the Book of Proverbs and underline all the passages which deal with choices and decision making.

4 Youth and Morality

Finally, brethren, whatsoever things are true, whatsoever things are honest, whatsoever things are just, whatsoever things are pure, whatsoever things are lovely, whatsoever things are of good report; if there be any virtue, and if there be any praise, think on these things.

Philippians 4:8

Start With the Scriptures

I Corinthians 3:16-17; 6:9-20
II Corinthians 6:14-18; 7:1
I Thessalonians 4:3-5
II Timothy 2:19-22

When we see or hear the word *morality*, we automatically link it with the term "sex" or "sexual." But let us take a look at the life of Joseph and others to see that morality includes not only our sexual behavior, but all areas of our lives.

Young people often struggle with the decision of where to establish the moral boundaries that they will follow throughout their lives. It is important to have strong convictions and a made-up mind as to what our personal "standards" are. With firmly defined morals we can live a much more worry-free life because we know our limits; we are not bouncing back and forth wondering what is right, wrong, acceptable or unacceptable. If we have established limits before we face a situation, then we will be more likely to stand up for what is right. The devil will not be able to play havoc with our staunch convictions.

From Sonship to Slavery

The life of Joseph probably started like that of many other boys of his time. He was one of many children and had his share of responsibilities, but he was also the favored son. This greatly angered his older brothers. There was no way for his father to hide his intense love for Joseph, and being young Joseph probably enjoyed the extra attention.

Joseph was in a situation in his life that he probably could not comprehend. He knew that his brothers did not lavish him with love, but who would dare to think that they would even consider killing him? But this was indeed the brothers' plan—all except for Reuben who pled not to kill Joseph. When Joseph arrived where the brothers were, they took and cast him into a dry pit. Now they had him! All they needed to do now was decide how and who would do away with him.

As they sat down to a meal they glanced across the field and beheld a company of traders coming their way. What a perfect answer to their situation. They could just sell Joseph. This way they could appease Reuben by not killing their younger brother and at the same time they would have Joseph off their hands for good. As a bonus they would have a little money with which to have some fun.

What would they tell their father? They knew this would be the hardest part because Jacob had loved

Joseph so much. Together they thought up the ideal story. They dipped Joseph's handmade coat into the blood of a goat and told their father that they had found the coat and that evidently some wild animal must have killed Joseph.

When Jacob heard the news and saw the coat, he tore his clothes, put on sackcloth and mourned for his son.

During this span of time Joseph had been sold again—not just to another family, but to a special family. Joseph was sold to Potiphar, who was an officer of Pharaoh.

In just a few short days Joseph's life had taken a complete turnabout. From the pampered, favored son of a loving father, Joseph became a slave.

From Prosperity to Prison

Joseph was taken to Egypt, but the Lord was with him and blessed him. Potiphar saw that all things which Joseph had prospered, so he made Joseph overseer of all his belongings.

Joseph was a handsome man and Potiphar's wife began to take notice. (See Genesis 39:6-7.) Soon she began asking Joseph to commit adultery with her. This happened not only once, but many times. Genesis 39:10 reveals that she spoke to Joseph day by day, but he did not heed or give in to her. Joseph, as a young man, had evidently already committed himself to some basic principles of decency and godliness. Without a commitment it would have been easy to succumb to the temptation that Potiphar's wife put before him every day.

Philippians 4:8 teaches that we should think on things that are pure. Wholesome thinking helps to guard our minds against sin. Any Christian who has fallen into sin probably first fantasized about doing things that are improper. This is not to say that all evil thoughts are fantasy or even willful sin. We are all human and have thoughts at times that are not pleasing to God. But we must put evil thoughts out of our minds, and the best way to do this is to begin thinking about things that are pure and holy.

Just because we do what is right is not a guarantee that life will always be just as we think it should be. Righteous conduct may sometimes have no apparent benefits immediately. Because Joseph refused Potiphar's wife, she lied about him to his master. As he fled from her, Joseph lost his garment which was presented to Potiphar as evidence of his supposed misconduct.

Potiphar was angered and ordered Joseph put into prison. Joseph was put where the king's prisoners were kept. It looked like everything bad that could happen was happening. Where was God now? After Joseph had kept his integrity and had refused to defile his earthly temple, he wound up in prison. But Joseph had a dream that kept his faith intact.

Every Christian needs an experience and commitment to God that he can look back to in a dark time when everything is seemingly going wrong. The Lord had not forsaken Joseph but was only leading him through some fires of testing.

The keeper of the prison was impressed with Joseph and put him over all the other prisoners. Joseph earned his trust and it was obvious that the blessings of the Lord were upon him.

Later Pharaoh became angry with the chief baker and chief butler and threw them into prison with Joseph. One night both the baker and butler had a dream.

The baker and butler were very disturbed because they did not know the meaning of the dreams. What a wonderful opportunity for Joseph to flex his spiritual muscles. God revealed to Joseph the interpretations. For the baker, his dream meant death.

But the butler was to be restored to his former position.

Joseph requested the butler to remember him when he was restored, but once freed from prison, the butler forgot. If placed in the predicament of Joseph, many modern Christians would probably have long been thinking that there was no end to their suffering and that God had forgotten them. But Joseph had a dream; he clung to his commitment and trust in God.

From Prison to Palace

Two years passed from the time the butler had been restored to his position. Joseph remained forgotten in the prison until God caused Pharaoh to dream two related dreams. When Pharaoh awoke from his sleep he was very troubled. Calling for all the magicians and wise men in the land, he sought for the interpretation of his dreams, but no one could interpret them.

Then the butler remembered what had happened to himself and the baker in the prison. He told these things to Pharaoh and Joseph was called to be brought quickly out of prison.

Even after being forgotten in the prison for two years Joseph's faith in God had not weakened. Genesis 41:16 reveals that Joseph was sure that God would give the answer. He assured the ruler that God would "give Pharaoh an answer of peace." There was no hesitation in Joseph's trust in and commitment to his God.

Joseph said to Pharaoh that God had shown him what was soon to happen. They would have seven years of plenty throughout the land, then seven years of famine that would deplete the resources of the land. Pharaoh was admonished to find a wise man and set him over Egypt. This man should collect twenty percent of the produce during the years of plenty and store it so there would be enough food during the years of famine.

Seeing that no one else was as wise as Joseph, Pharaoh chose Joseph for the position he had proposed. Joseph was set up as second only to Pharaoh himself in all of the kingdom. God's ways are so far above our ways!

From Famine to Fortune

About twenty years had passed since Joseph was sold into slavery by his brothers. When due to the famine Joseph's brothers came seeking food, it was before Joseph they bowed. Although they did not recognize Joseph, he recognized them. What a change of events! The ones who so hated their brother that they sold him into the hands of strangers, not caring if he lived or died, were now in his hands of judgment.

In this sense Joseph is a perfect picture of Christ. Many times people get themselves into trouble because they are unwilling to live disciplined, holy lives. Then when they see that they cannot help themselves, they came to God for Him to rescue them. So it was with Joseph and his brothers.

Had Joseph not maintained such a strong desire for what is right, he would have viewed the situation as his turn for revenge. But because he had maintained his integrity with God, he did his brothers no harm. Joseph could have had his brothers slain as they had once wished him, but he held to the dream that was being fulfilled before his eyes.

What a way God has to bring to pass His ultimate plan. The brothers who had done away with their brother, ultimately because of his dream, lived to see him again and the dream fulfilled. Joseph possessed the moral integrity to let God be the avenger. Perhaps we should ask ourselves if we have that kind of integrity.

The Character of Joseph Examined

Morally upright. Throughout the life of Joseph he was a morally clean and upright person. What is morality? It is our standard of conduct, upright behavior or virtue. This affects every aspect of our daily lives—our performance on the job, our conduct on a date, the respect we show our parents, elders and superiors.

We should examine Joseph's standard of conduct. He was evidently a very good worker because Potiphar was so impressed with his performance that he turned all the responsibilities of his household over to him. God blessed everything that Joseph did. Even in prison Joseph was upright and obviously a good prisoner because he found favor in the sight of the prison keeper. Again, Joseph proved himself so well that the prison keeper placed him over all the other prisoners. God prospered him even in the prison.

Joseph's life is an example for us of how we should serve others. Our employer deserves our very best efforts on the job. A Christian should never take advantage of the person or company which employs him. Time pledged to someone else deserves our highest standard of work.

What about our virtue, our moral uprightness? Joseph was morally pure even while facing constant temptation from Potiphar's wife. As a young man, it would have been easy for Joseph to have let the lust of the flesh overcome him. He would have had every excuse that a person could use to attempt to justify such behavior—he had a hard life, had been rejected by ones that he loved, could have felt forgotten by God and the list goes on. But Joseph had a higher vision than just the pleasure presented to him for a moment.

How do we behave when there is no one around to know what we are doing? Do we have strong enough principles to preserve us when we think no one else would ever find out?

A Christian should never entertain evil or immoral thoughts. If a person allows such thoughts to linger in their minds, they will soon blossom and that person will find himself in a tempting position to yield to his thoughts.

King David is an example. At an earlier time in his life he had strong principles and was a man "after God's own heart," but evidently he started entertaining immoral thoughts. At a time when kings were in battle, David was at home taking it easy. While strolling on his rooftop, he happened to see beautiful Bathsheba as she bathed, and he lusted after her. Had he immediately turned away and refused to allow that lust to increase, he could have rejected the temptation of Satan. But he remained, watching her bathe, and he soon lost control of his desires.

One of a person's primary guards against immorality is that he never allows himself to be in a situation that could get out of hand. We are responsible for our own actions. If we lose control of our body, we are the one to blame. We cannot shift that responsibility to someone else. We must be honest enough with ourselves to realize that we are accountable for our actions, and the best way to keep a guard up is to start with good basic principles and convictions. This will keep us out of questionable situations. The Bible teaches us to abstain from all appearance of evil (I Thessalonians 5:22). If we follow this rule it will help us to protect ourselves against the enticements of Satan.

The Spiritual Truths of Joseph's Life

What can be done if we work with God in the task before us? The achievements and possibilities of our lives are without limits if we work with God. To some it may have seemed that Joseph would never reach the fulfillment of his dream, but every obstacle turned into a "stepping stone."

Anyone that has lived for God any length of time has been through times when he probably wondered if God knew that he still existed. But years later a person can look back and see how God was leading and preparing him for greater victories and accomplishments.

Men who do evil always live with guilt. Joseph's brothers are a prime example of individuals living with guilt. It had been twenty years since they had sold their younger brother. But as they stood before this "foreign" governor asking for food, they were talking among themselves about how they had wronged Joseph and how they were possibly experiencing the judgment of God for their sin.

Getting rid of Joseph evidently had not solved the brothers' problems with uncontrolled emotions as perhaps they had previously thought. They had only traded hatred for guilt. But Joseph, the one who had been treated so wrongfully, was not full of hatred and revenge—only full of gratitude at seeing his father and family again.

It is always rewarding in the end to be clean, pure and moral. We can face ourselves every day with a clear conscience knowing we have kept our earthly temple wholesome before God. We do not have to wake up in the morning wondering what we might have said or done in a drunken stupor the night before, but we can "present ourselves a living sacrifice, acceptable to God." People who choose to live selfishly and only for today will face their decision one day in the future with ruined lives and broken hearts.

The choice of morality is ours. Christians cannot live their lives "straddling the fence" of commitment. There is a choice to make and it will be made. We will either be good or bad, holy or unholy, moral or immoral. Some people tend to think that they can just drift day by day and take life as it comes. But Christians are not able to do this successfully. There are times when a person is forced to make choices between right and wrong. (See chapter three.)

God is with us even in the darkest hour. Joseph had numerous opportunities to feel that God had deserted him, but his faith remained strong and intact. Apparently, Joseph never wanted to give up even though he spent many years forgotten by others. God, however, never forgot him. Instead God blessed everything Joseph did.

God was also with Esther when she went before the king without permission. This could have meant immediate death. Instead the king gave her favor and allowed her to come into the royal court.

The truth of Romans 8:28. The Apostle Paul in his letter to the Romans explicitly declared that "all things work together for good to them that love God, to them who are the called according to his purpose" (Romans 8:28). Joseph's life is perhaps a perfect example of this verse of Scripture.

Joseph went from being a beloved son, to a hated brother, a slave, accused as a rapist, a prisoner and finally a governor, second only to the Pharaoh himself. God had His hand on Joseph through every day of his life. It was all working to the fulfillment of a dream which was a prophecy from God.

At the beginning Joseph did not know where all he would travel to fulfill this dream and all the traps Satan would set trying to sidetrack him. But with one goal in mind, Joseph must have told God, "Have dream, will travel," because that is certainly what he did. He set his affections on God and followed after the dream to which he had anchored his life.

The protection and strength of standards. Sometimes people grumble and complain because of the standards Pentecostals hold dear, thinking that the standards keep them from having a good time and enjoying life. But the opposite is true. It is the clean living that allows us to have a clear conscience and enjoy the abundant life God has given us to the fullest possible extent. What a relief it is to know that if Jesus Christ were to return today for His church, we would be ready to meet Him in peace.

A minister once said that as a young boy, his family was very poor. Having very little material possessions, they never worried about locking the doors on the house. Later as they "moved up in the world" and accumulated some valuable possessions, they had to be careful to see that their possessions were secured. The more a person possesses, the more effort he will expend to protect those things.

The same reasoning is true with our souls. When we have nothing in our hearts, we really do not care how we live. But when we receive God's most precious gift, the Holy Ghost, we put some "locks" on our hearts. These locks, which are standards of holiness by which we secure our lives, cause us to keep a clean temple, to dress modestly, and to present our bodies a living sacrifice, holy and acceptable unto God. If we are living our best for God we do not consider these moral boundaries a restraint, but a support to assist us while fleeing youthful lusts.

Test Your Knowledge

1. What place did Joseph occupy in his father's heart?

2. What happening caused Joseph's brothers' anger to increase toward him?

3. How did Jacob react when Joseph told his dream?

4. What were the brothers' first intentions in doing away with Joseph and who intervened?

5. To whom did the traders sell Joseph?

6. Was Potiphar's wife a godly lady?

7. What did Potiphar's wife do to Joseph?

8. Was Esther afraid to stand up against her peers?

9. What is the purpose of standards of morality?

10. Who pays in the end if we act immorally, and why?

Apply Your Knowledge

Some young people are morally "bankrupt." Take time now to determine your personal standing. Do you abound in moral strength? What are you doing to strengthen yourself in your weaker areas?

Expand Your Knowledge

Study the lives of Daniel, Esther, and the three Hebrew children. These people exemplified high morals and strong characters. Use the good things that you learn from them and apply them to your personal situation.

5. Youth and Study

Study to shew thyself approved unto God, a workman that needeth not to be ashamed, rightly dividing the word of truth.

II Timothy 2:15

Start With the Scriptures

Deuteronomy 17:19 Acts 17:11
Isaiah 34:16 Romans 15:4
Revelation 1:3

"Eat all of your spinach," Mom said. "Don't you want to grow up to be big and strong like your dad?"

As the boy sat staring at that distasteful green mound, he wondered why things that are good for him are usually unpleasant. At times they seem totally unbearable!

Things we do not enjoy are usually good for us. Things we love to do are often harmful. Right? Wrong! It really boils down to our attitude. The subject of this chapter is the value of study. Studying is an exercise in self-discipline, but studying can be enjoyable when approached with the right attitude.

Why Study?

"Why study? I'm not going to be a professor," Joe said as he headed out the door, ball glove in hand. Joe figured he could pass with average grades and go on to find an on-the-job training opportunity.

For Mary, study seemed futile. Her ambition was to be a housewife and mother. How could being a good student prepare her to make beds, clean house and raise children?

"If I were going to be a preacher, I might study my Bible, but that's why I go to church. I leave the studying up to my pastor and the listening up to me."

These are typical attitudes of people who deplore the discipline of study. They are asking, "Why study?" The following reasons should help to answer this question.

We study to please God. Historically, some groups of Christians have expressed a fear of knowledge. To them, knowledge was the forbidden fruit that destroyed Adam and Eve. On the contrary, the Bible encourages the pursuit of knowledge (Proverbs 2:1-12). In fact, the only knowledge condemned by the Scriptures is the intimate knowledge of evil. "I would have you wise unto that which is good, and simple concerning evil" (Romans 16:19). We are instructed to be aware of what is taking place in the world around us (Ephesians 5:15). Whatever we do, we are to do it with all of our hearts as unto the Lord (Colossians 3:23).

God expects us to study. Jesus chided the accusing Pharisees in Matthew 12:3 by asking, "Have ye not read what David did. . . ." In verse five He continued by saying, "Or have ye not read in the law. . . ." Jesus rebuked this group of religious experts because they were living by hearsay and man's opinions without studying the Scriptures for themselves. In areas of spirituality, we are to search the Scriptures because they hold the answers to eternal life (John 5:39). Philippians 4:8 encourages us to think! God is pleased when we study.

It is hard for us to imagine Jesus failing a test because He did not study or because He skipped school for no reason. Would we respect the Apostle Paul if we knew that he slept at the feet of Gamaliel, his teacher? Paul was a student of life. He knew the teachings of philosophers in his day. In Athens, where people spent their time in nothing else but to tell or to hear some new thing, Paul called on past study. He quoted fragments of philosophy in order to make known the unknown God—Jesus Christ!

The Bible teaches us to love God with our mind (Matthew 22:37). We are accountable to God as stewards of our talents and intellect. We study to please God.

We study to reflect the excellence of God. In all of creation, God displays His excellent greatness. We are no exception. God created us with the potential for excellence. If God can be glorified in ignorance, how much more in knowledge. Why worship the Lord with sloppiness when He deserves excellence!

It is a fact that God works through, and often in spite of, our limitations. If God gave a song to a person who only knew three chords on the piano, then the song God gave would only have three chords. The majesty and excellence of God, however, deserves more than mediocrity from our lives. We should apply ourselves to study so that we can reflect the excellence of God with our minds.

We study to develop discipline in our character. The military holds the opinion that imposed discipline becomes self-discipline. They induct a civilian and in six weeks develop a soldier. Although boot camp is not war, it prepares a man for war. One great purpose of study is to develop the discipline we need to be successful in life.

"It is good for a man that he bear the yoke in his youth" (Lamentations 3:27). The only way to develop discipline is to submit to discipline and accept responsibility. Bearing the yoke of disciplined study in our youth will develop diligence in our character for all of our lives. We study because it will pay off in character qualities that will make us successful.

We study to build a broad base for our future. A man of preparation is a man of opportunity. Although some areas of study may seem unimportant to our personal goals, they are building our life message. It is more important to make a life than to make a living. Much of the knowledge we gain through study is best applied to our own personal development. Knowledge can hone our "people skills" and make us a valuable asset to any church or company.

A person with only one skill lives in jeopardy. Should that occupation become obsolete, that person is left jobless. The more we are prepared to face the future, the more opportunities we will have for a fulfilling and rewarding life. The great scientist, Einstein, put it well. "It is essential that the student acquire an understanding of and a lively feeling for values. He must acquire a vivid sense of the beautiful and of the morally good. Otherwise, he, with his specialized knowledge, more closely resembles a well-trained dog than a harmoniously developed person." We study to build a broad base for our future.

In summary of the reasons given why we study:
- We study to please God.
- God expects us to study.
- We study to reflect the excellence of God.

- We study to develop discipline in our character.
- We study to build a broad base for our future.

The Value of Study

Ignorance is weakness; knowledge is power. Knowledge elevates our view of life and enables us to enjoy the advantage of a broader perspective. Someone said that ignorance is bliss. In some cases that may be true, but most often ignorance is imprisonment. Ignorance writes most of a person's life "script." Menial pay, limited associates, restricted activities, and the prospect of identical futures for our offspring are the "story line."

Knowledge is power because it offers us alternatives. Salvation is based on the knowledge of God's offer of salvation and a new life. The knowledge of God says we have a choice; we can have eternal life. Ignorance condemns, confines, and kills the hopes of a happy life. "If the ax is dull, and one does not sharpen the edge, then he must use more strength; but wisdom brings success" (Ecclesiastes 10:10, *NKJV*). The obvious lesson of this verse is that the less we know, the more effort we must exert in life. The slogan of one grocery store chain is "work smarter, not harder." The aim of study is increased knowledge, and knowledge is power. Knowledge saves needed strength and is often its own reward.

While recently planning a trip, one man learned from the newspaper that through an airline's special fare, he could fly to his destination more economically than he could drive. What did that knowledge do? It saved time, physical energy, wear and tear on his car, and allowed him to see the world from a higher (30,000 feet) perspective. The time taken to study may cost; but it always pays handsomely.

Spiritually speaking, time spent in study of God's

Word is never wasted time. It is the wisest investment a person can make. Ignorance of the Bible means taking a trip through life without referring to the road map. One young person spent many days studying the Book of Proverbs. Its thirty-one chapters can be read on a daily basis and the entire book completed in one month. That book of wisdom was invaluable to him as he faced the unexpected twists, turns, and events of life. He is thankful for the internal guiding system that the study of Proverbs gave him.

"Do you see a man who excels in his work? He will stand before kings; he will not stand before unknown men" (Proverbs 22:29, *NKJV*). One of the values of study is that it promotes advancement in life. As one deepens his knowledge, he will broaden his influence. Excelling in whatever he does will bring promotion in time.

We must not be discouraged by those who seem to be fast-starters in life. They may have more natural ability, higher intellect, and earlier opportunities. However, over a longer period, the person who applies himself to study will excel. Gifted individuals who do not apply themselves to study may shine brighter, but they burn out sooner than the consecrated person who continues to work and study diligently. The value of study is not always obvious over the short term. It is over the long term that the difference is clear.

A final value of study is in the witness we can be for Jesus Christ in our world. The finest, level-headed leaders in our world should come from the Christian community. The best thinkers should be those whose knowledge in every area of life is subordinated to the knowledge of the Word of God. When we apply ourselves to study the Word of God and other knowledge useful in life, we will emerge as the leaders in our communities. The value of study is the witness we can be for Jesus Christ when we represent Him to our world.

How to Study

The creative genius who made human minds did not stamp them out of a mold. Because we are all unique individuals, we must learn how we function best. To study effectively, we need to learn how our mind works.

A major factor affecting study is confidence. Admittedly, when we begin a project we may experience some apprehension. Our lack of confidence affects our aggressiveness in study. Confidence comes through competence. *Competence* is defined as "the ability to function effectively." As we study and gain understanding of the facts, our apprehension dissipates and our competence increases. The more skilled we are, the more confident we become. Learning how to study will make us better students.

The following are tips to use in study.

Find the best time. Some people are larks and prefer to rise early and study. Others are owls and enjoy studying at night. Although the morning hours are generally best because we are rested, we should find the time that best suits us.

Find the best place. Some people can study at a public library. Although it is not totally quiet, they can work undisturbed. We function best without interruptions. Our prime place to study is in an interruption-free environment. It may be our room, the church prayer room, or a quiet spot outdoors. We must make the effort to get to the place where we can best think and study.

Pray for help. Before beginning any study project, spiritual or secular, we should ask for divine assistance. God is the ultimate source of knowledge. He will provide the strength needed to learn from study.

Stick with it. We should not allow the "itchy-feet" syndrome to cut study time short. We must force ourselves to stay with it until we are finished. By nature, we may not tend to be a student. Students are not born; they are made through discipline.

Take breaks. Depending on one's stamina, it is best to take breaks every 45-60 minutes. Standing up, stretching, and taking five minutes to rest the mind are helpful breaks. Then, we get back down to the business of study.

Have a strategy. In the book, *Making the Most of Your Mind,* Stephen Douglass and Lee Roddy share a widely-used, four-point Bible-study approach. It can be applied to study of various types of material.

- Observe. (What do we see?) What is the theme of the material? What key words are used? Who are the people involved?
- Interpret. (What does it mean?) What is the meaning of the words used? What conclusions can we draw from the passage? Can we paraphrase what is said? Are any hard questions raised?
- Apply. (What does it mean to us?) Where do our lives not fully conform to the passage? How can we apply the concepts to our own lives?
- Correlate. (Where does it fit?) How does this relate to other passages we have read? We may try to simplify and express the main ideas in order to get a clearer mental picture of the concepts. We can think through how our lives will be changed as a result of this new information.

Richard Foster, in *Celebration of Discipline,* offers four steps of study.

- Repetition. Repetition is a way of regularly channeling the mind in a specific direction, thus ingraining habits of thought.
- Concentration. Concentration centers the mind. It focuses the attention on the thing being studied.

- Comprehension. This step leads to insight and discernment. It provides the basis for the true perception of reality.
- Reflection. To reflect and ruminate leads us to an inner reality of what we are studying. We come to understand not only our subject matter, but ourselves. Reflection gives significance to what we are studying.

Applying Knowledge to Life

We have all encountered people with head knowledge but little common sense. Their intellectual insights have never transferred into real life. Knowledge is not to be showcased and flaunted. Primarily, it should affect the quality of our lives. It should make us better people.

Wisdom is the right application of knowledge in moral and spiritual matters. Wisdom is seeing life from God's point of view. Being a student of the Scriptures and of life can give a person wisdom beyond his years. When we study the wisdom of the ages, God's Word, we have an edge in life. Approaching life's situations with the knowledge gained from diligent study, we graduate above foolish mistakes. We can even "skip" many of the lessons others learn only by mistake.

Mark Twain said that "the man who can read and doesn't is no better off than the man who can't read." It is also true that if a person studies and gains knowledge, yet does not apply it to his life, he is no better off than the person who is void of knowledge.

The ultimate value of study is in a changed life. We are advantaged if we apply ourselves to study and then apply our studies to life.

Test Your Knowledge

1. The key to enjoying the discipline of study is having the right _____.
2. List five reasons why we should study.
   a. _____
   b. _____
   c. _____
   d. _____
   e. _____
3. Knowledge is power because it offers us
   _____.
4. The great value of study is made obvious over the _____.
5. Confidence comes through _____, which is the ability to _____ effectively.
6. List six tips for studying.
   a. _____
   b. _____
   c. _____
   d. _____
   e. _____
   f. _____
7. Wisdom is seeing life from _____.
8. The ultimate value of study is in a _____ life.
9. The Bible only condemns the knowledge of _____ .
10. The United States military holds the opinion the _____ discipline becomes _____ discipline.
11. A man of _____ is a man of _____.
12. _____ is the biblical book of wisdom.

Apply Your Knowledge

How good are your study habits? Do you have a regular study time? See how you measure up to the six tips for studying.

Now, make a plan to do better. Using those six tips, plan your next study session:
1. Time _____
2. Place_____
3. Prayer _____
4. Did I stick with it? _____
5. Did I take breaks?_____
6. What was my strategy? _____

Plan a study of the Book of Proverbs, beginning with the first day of next month. As you read, highlight verses you want to memorize and apply to your life.

Expand Your Knowledge

To expand your knowledge in the area of study, refer to the following books:
1. Douglass, Stephen B. and Roddy, Lee, *Making the Most of Your Mind*. Campus Crusade for Christ, San Bernardino, CA, 1983.
2. Foster, Richard J., *Celebration of Discipline*. Harper & Row Publishers, San Francisco, CA, 1978.
3. Narramore, Clyde M., *How to Study and be Successful in School*, Zondervan Publishing House, Grand Rapids, MI, 1977.
4. White, Jerry, *Making the Grade*, NavPress, Colorado Springs, CO, 1980.

Youth and Submission 6

Submitting yourselves one to another in the fear of the Lord.

Ephesians 5:21

Start With the Scriptures

II Kings 1-4	Luke 1:26-38
II Chronicles 29:23-25	Luke 2:51-52
Matthew 6:9-13	Romans 6:13
Matthew 26:36-46	Hebrews 13:17

Submission Defined

Divinely interwoven into the Word of God are some of the greatest secrets of success man has ever known. Buried deep in the sacred treasure chest of the Scriptures one may find keys to happiness, peace, and joy that will never be found in any other source.

These gems of truth, however, will never be found by simply lifting the lid and taking a quick glance, for on the surface one can see only the disciplines that are unfavorable to our human nature, such as submission, obedience, and humility. Many will take one look and close the lid, for carnal thinking tells us that true happiness can never be found in self-abasement. Human nature strongly opposes the idea that true peace can be found in the giving of ourselves for others. Sadly enough, thousands will continue this trek called life in a state of confusion and frustration because they never realized that buried under the seemingly rigid disciplines in the Word of God are the sparkling jewels of truth that will bring true fulfillment to a person's life.

We live in a power-hungry society. The lives of so many people today are consumed with only one goal and that is to succeed no matter what the cost. In their quest for greatness, however, it seems that they have forgotten some important God-given principles. Is wealth the true sign of greatness in a person's life? Can it be found in the position that he holds in his or her company? Can a person's nobility be gauged by his or her social standing? The answer to all of these questions, of course, is no. According to the Scriptures, the key to true greatness in God's eyes can be summed up in one word—submission.

Submission, we ask? That seems like such a contradiction! However, the Bible is full of paradoxes. It seems impossible to us that strength can be found in weakness (II Corinthians 12:9), or that joy can be found in tears (Psalm 126:5-6). Paul gave us the answer in I Corinthians 1:27, "But God hath chosen the foolish things of the world to confound the wise; and God hath chosen the weak things of the world to confound the things which are mighty."

In order to truly understand submission we must analyze it from a godly standpoint.

As a preface to the remainder of this chapter let

us take a close look at this word *submission.* What does it literally mean? *Strong's Exhaustive Dictionary of the New Testament* briefly defines the word in this manner: "to be under obedience." For many people this word is connected to weakness, and their pre-conceived ideas tell them that submission is something that God ordained strictly for women to practice in the marriage relationship. Not so! Submission to God is not a sign of weakness, but a sign of obedience to His will.

According to the prophets Ezekiel and Isaiah, the original sin in the universe was pride. Pride was found in Lucifer when he declared that he would be like the Most High. Because of this pride, Lucifer became Satan and was cast out of heaven. Pride is the origin of all sin and always results from lack of submission.

The only thing in the entire universe not directly controlled by God is the human will. God gave mankind a choice of whom they would worship. But in order to worship, a man must submit his will. To never submit is to be proud and "pride goeth before destruction, and an haughty spirit before a fall" (Proverbs 16:18). An unsubmitted life will always be destroyed.

It has always been God's plan for humans to worship Him of their own volition. When God created man He instilled in him the power and the responsibility to choose between right and wrong. When Adam and Eve were placed in the Garden of Eden, they were immediately required to make a choice. Would they choose to submit to God's will and not eat of the forbidden fruit, or would they surrender to the ever-present force of evil that continually tells man that he is superior to God's design? It is a sad but familiar story, and we know it only too well. We are still experiencing the adverse effects of man's initial refusal to submit to God's will.

This account also helps us to understand better the question of why God has deemed submission so important when fulfilling His master plan. Where would we be today if Adam and Eve had chosen to obey God instead of Satan? The answer to that question is pure speculation, of course, but this much is sure—God's plan is always best!

A person may wonder what it would be like to really "do his own thing," to be so independent that he did not have to answer to anyone. He may picture the following scene in his mind. He approaches a major intersection in his city and notices that the traffic light is changing to red. He instinctively reaches out his foot to apply the brakes when suddenly it occurs to him that he is an adult! He is of legal age and he has the power to make his own decisions. How preposterous to think that he, an intelligent, responsible human being, must cater to the whims of an electronic safety guard that does not even have the power to enforce its own commands! With his new found independence proudly leading the way, he hits the accelerator and shoots confidently into the stream of traffic, oblivious to the cacophony of horns, squealing tires, and shouts.

He may be lucky enough to avoid any vehicles coming through the intersection from the opposite directions, but chances are he will wind up in an accident, affecting not only himself, but others around him.

Is this a silly supposition? Maybe so, but there are those who are applying this same principle of dominance in their everyday lives. Disregarding all warning signs either from God's Word or from those in authority, they charge into situations that eventually wind up hurting not only themselves, but others also. Why? Simply because they never learned to submit to God's plan for their lives.

Why Submission to God Is Important

Our hearts are saddened by the testimony of the prophet Jeremiah concerning Israel, when he lamented, "This hath been thy manner from thy youth, that thou obeyedst not my voice" (Jeremiah 22:21). God can greatly use a young person who learns the beauty of submission, but one who adopts an attitude of ascendancy is destined for a life of spiritual barrenness. But how different the testimony of young Samuel, who gave his heart to God at an early age: "And the child Samuel ministered unto the LORD before Eli" (I Samuel 3:1).

One of the most beautiful portraits of submission we could ever study is found in II Kings 1-2. The prophet Elijah had just returned from Horeb, where God had encouraged him and redefined his mission. Passing through Abel-Meholah, Elijah spotted a young man plowing in the field who was, of course, later identified as Elisha. The Bible does not record a single word passing between the two of them; it simply says that Elijah cast his mantle upon Elisha, identifying Elisha as his successor. In the course of that simple act, the realization struck Elisha that he would be the next prophet of Israel.

This incident gives us candid insight into the spiritual attitude of Elisha. Had he not had a willing heart, tuned in and sensitive to the will of God, he probably would have passed Elijah off as a daft old man. Instead, he realized that in receiving Elijah's mantle he was being ordained as God's instrument to speak to His people.

Here is where the true test of Elisha's submissive spirit begins. More than likely, he was a normal young man with friends, social interests, and maybe even romantic attachments. However, one of the unique elements about Elisha's response lies in the fact that he never once asked to say goodbye to friends and acquaintances. His eagerness to serve was indicated by his submissiveness; even an attitude of submissiveness is evidenced in his desire to pay honor to his parents. Embarking on a life of service and total dedication, Elisha was more than eager to sacrifice his own desires.

The story does not end there, however, for there is great spiritual reward achieved by living a life of submission. When the twilight years of Elijah's life approached, he invited Elisha to make any request of him. Disregarding riches and worldly fame, Elisha simply asked for a double portion of the power that was demonstrated through Elijah. In accordance with the old prophet's instructions Elisha dogged his footsteps until the elder was received up into heaven by fiery chariots.

The young prophet must have fairly shook with a combination of excitement and apprehension as he draped the sacred mantle over his shoulders. Elisha realized that it was now time to put his faith to the test. Would the years of unselfish service and intense devotion, living in the shadow of another man's ministry, now bring reward? With one mighty burst of faith, Elisha smote the waters of the rushing Jordan River, and just as they had done moments before, they parted so that the prophet walked over on dry ground.

Possibly the only thoughts in Elisha's mind as he crossed the dry river bed were ones of thankfulness that he had learned to submit at an early age. Consequently, he realized the fulfillment of his request of a double portion by performing twice the number of miracles that his mentor, Elijah, had performed during his earthly ministry. Coincidence? Not really. Just the rewards of a life of submission to God's will.

How Jesus Submitted

When studying the principle of submission we cannot overlook the embodiment of all godly traits and characteristics—the man Christ Jesus. John revealed to us in John 1:14, "And the Word was made flesh, and dwelt among us." Paul further enlightened us when he wrote, "God was manifest in the flesh" (I Timothy 3:16). The Scriptures irrevocably state that Jesus Christ was actually God robed in the flesh.

But when Jesus came to earth to perform His redemptive work, did He come in a show of power, wielding supernatural force, vowing to clean up the world with one sweep of His mighty scepter? Did He emerge on the world scene surrounded by multitudes of the heavenly host, ready to seize power and establish an earthly kingdom? Absolutely not! Possibly if He had, many more would have followed Him, but for the wrong reason. He chose to assume the form of a servant. The true purpose of the ministry of Christ is revealed in Matthew 20:28; "Even as the Son of man came not to be ministered unto, but to minister, and to give his life a ransom for many." What a beautiful testimony of our perfect example! When studying His life we can see that from His entrance into the world, His every action was dedicated to fulfilling this assignment.

The attitude of the child Jesus is clearly portrayed in Luke 2:51: "And he went down with them, and came to Nazareth, and was subject unto them." The principle of submission was so important in God's overall plan that even when He took on the form of man He deemed it necessary to place Himself under the authority of earthly parents.

In sharing the exemplary Lord's Prayer with the disciples, Jesus once again confirms His unerring belief in submission by praying that the Father's will be done on earth as it is in heaven. One need only look at nature to see a system that is in perfect order and harmony with the Creator. The stars in the sky never deviate from the Father's will; they twinkle and shine whenever He commands. The leaves on the trees never complain about changing colors in the autumn, they simply acquiesce in resplendent beauty.

The only creature that God ever brought into existence that is not totally subordinate to His will is man. Consequently, the only way for God's will to totally be done on earth as it is in heaven is for us to surrender our emotions, feelings, desires, and will to the will of the Father. This is possibly the most difficult task known to man, the surrender of self-will.

However, one should not feel as if he is the first to face this dilemma, or that it is an impossible mission to accomplish. We have only to trace the steps of Jesus a little farther down the path of destiny to find Him in a very unpleasant situation. Gone are the screaming worshipers that lined the road leading into Jerusalem. Gone are the thankful recipients of His healing virtue. The divinity and humanity which were both incarnate in Jesus struggled for control as He agonized in the Garden of Gethsemane. With Jesus' earthly ministry approaching completion, Satan did everything within his power to thwart the plan of God.

Dying a gruesome death is not a pleasant experience, no matter how worthy the cause. To bring the flesh under subjection to the Spirit was a monumental task and it was not completed without great physical and spiritual agony. While wrestling with His human emotions and fears, His body was wracked with sobs and tears streamed down His contorted face to mingle with the sweat that sheathed His entire body. Although the vast majority of the world never knew it until much later, the most crucial life-changing battle to ever take place in the course of human history was in progress.

The beautiful epilogue to this story is that after hours of groaning and agonizing, Jesus walked out of the garden, the Spirit leading the way while the flesh followed meekly behind. Submission to God's plan had once again provided means whereby mankind could enjoy great spiritual benefits.

Submission in Your Life

We have studied the effects of submission in the lives of two great men of the Bible, but is submission a thing of the past? Was it designed specifically for those who lived under the Mosaic law? Are we that have experienced the liberating power of Jesus Christ now free from all authority? Submission is still God's plan for greatness.

Man has always desired to be great, and that desire within itself is not wrong, for it is a God-given desire. However, God's method of achieving greatness varies so greatly from our own that it is often difficult to accept. Man has become so self-sufficient that he often cannot grasp the thought of submitting to higher authority. We are reminded again that the concept of strength through weakness, or greatness through submission, is not perceived by human nature alone.

The Bible gives us candid insight not only into the need for submission, but also into the rewards of submission. "Submit yourselves therefore to God. Resist the devil, and he will flee from you" (James 4:7). "No man can serve two masters: for either he will hate the one, and love the other; or else he will hold to the one, and despise the other. Ye cannot serve God and mammon" (Matthew 6:24). Possibly one of the most important principles we can learn in our walk with God is this—submission to one authority automatically insures resistance to the opposing authority.

Many Christians erroneously feel that they have the power within themselves to withstand the forces of evil. They misinterpret I John 4:4 to read, "greater are ye than he that is in the world." In doing so they unsuccessfully try to combat the wiles of the devil and miserably fail. I John 4:4 accurately reads, "Ye are of God, little children, and have overcome them: because greater is he that is in you, than he that is in the world." According to the Scriptures it is the Spirit of God that dwells in us that makes us victorious over sin.

To challenge the devil without being filled with the Spirit would be like going bear hunting with an empty gun! When we are looking down the barrel of a useless piece of steel, a thousand pounds of charging, snarling fury drawing closer by the second, the need for better preparation becomes suddenly evident! Many folks are on a "devil hunt" without the proper ammunition. When it comes to a showdown they will wish they had prepared properly by totally submitting to God.

When a person always seems to have trouble in his walk with God, oftentimes the trouble can be traced to a lack of submission. We cannot fight the battle on our own; we must have divine help. The beauty of this principle is that God is eagerly awaiting our request for assistance. When we stop fighting the battle and turn it over to Him, we can stand still and see the salvation of the Lord.

Paul wrote in Romans 6:13 to "Neither yield ye your members as instruments of unrighteousness unto sin: but yield yourselves unto God, as those that are alive from the dead, and your members as instruments of righteousness unto God." By yielding our bodies a living sacrifice we leave the realm of the spiritually "dead" and become alive in Christ.

Authority Figures for Submission

We have discussed the requirements and rewards of submission; now let us consider another vital aspect of submission. One question that is important to us all is, "To whom must I submit?" One person made this statement, "No man is going to tell me what to do!" Of course, the implication was that he answered only to God, but, is it possible to reach that higher state of perfection in which we are superior to human authority, and become accountable only to God? Absolutely not! Part of God's plan of submission includes responsibility to human administration.

According to the Scriptures the chain of authority may be established somewhat as follows:

- Submission to God.

"And he went a little farther, and fell on his face, and prayed, saying, O my Father, if it be possible, let this cup pass from me: nevertheless not as I will, but as thou wilt" (Matthew 26:39).

"Thy kingdom come. Thy will be done in earth, as it is in heaven" (Matthew 6:10).

- Submission to parents.

"Honour thy father and thy mother: that thy days may be long upon the land which the LORD thy God giveth thee" (Exodus 20:12).

"Children, obey your parents in all things: for this is well pleasing unto the Lord" (Colossians 3:20).

- Submission to church leaders.

"And I will give you pastors according to mine heart, which shall feed you with knowledge and understanding" (Jeremiah 3:15).

"Obey them that have the rule over you, and submit yourselves: for they watch for your souls, as they that must give account, that they may do it with joy, and not with grief: for that is unprofitable for you" (Hebrews 13:17).

- Submission to one another as brothers and sisters in Christ.

"Submitting yourselves one to another in the fear of God" (Ephesians 5:21).

"Likewise, ye younger, submit yourselves unto the elder. Yea, all of you be subject one to another, and be clothed with humility: for God resisteth the proud, and giveth grace to the humble" (I Peter 5:5).

- Submission to supervisors and authority at places of employment.

"As the cold of snow in the time of harvest, so is a faithful messenger to them that send him: for he refresheth the soul of his masters" (Proverbs 25:13).

"Let as many servants as are under the yoke count their own masters worthy of all honour, that the name of God and his doctrine be not blasphemed" (I Timothy 6:1).

- Submission to governmental authority.

"Submit yourselves to every ordinance of man for the Lord's sake: whether it be to the king as supreme; Or unto governors, as unto them that are sent by him for the punishment of evildoers, and for the praise of them that do well" (I Peter 2:13-14).

"Let every soul be subject unto the higher powers. For there is no power but of God: the powers that be are ordained of God" (Romans 13:1).

The need for submission in the life of a Christian is evident when illuminated by the light of the Scriptures. In a world that is influenced by the he-man concept of a hero, it is refreshing to realize that the key to true power and greatness is still found in submission to God.

Test Your Knowledge

1. The literal translation of the word *submission* is _____.

2. The original sin in heaven was _____

and was caused by lack of _____.

3. Elisha's _____ was the key to his following Elijah to be his successor.

4. The Bible says Jesus did not come to be _____ unto, but instead to _____.

5. The only way for God's will to be done is for a person to surrender his _____.

6. Submission to the cross brought _____ to humanity.

7. God always provides _____ to a person to submit to.

8. According to James 4:7, the key to resisting the devil is to _____.

9. When a person has trouble in Spirit living, often the problem can be traced to _____.

10. Examples of authority figures a person should submit to are _____, _____, _____, _____, _____.

Apply Your Knowledge

Think about the authority figure in your life to whom you have the most difficulty submitting. Evaluate the situation and analyze why you cannot submit your will. Are you afraid of harm? Is pride a problem? Do you believe God will honor your submission?

Evaluate your situation in view of the Scriptures and decide how Jesus would handle your problem.

Expand Your Knowledge

Complete a study of several major characters in the Bible and analyze where each did or did not display the spirit of submission in their lives. Summarize where these men failed or succeeded in their walk with God and purpose in your heart not to make their mistakes.

7 Youth and Witnessing

But ye shall receive power, after that the Holy Ghost is come upon you: and ye shall be witnesses unto me both in Jerusalem, and in all Judaea, and in Samaria, and unto the uttermost part of the earth.
Acts 1:8

Start With the Scriptures

II Kings 5
Luke 14:16-24
Acts 18:1-6, 24-28
II Corinthians 5:11

None of us knows what the Lord may be doing with our testimony. Sometimes God uses the words of common people to reach those with outstanding ability. This was true with Aquila and Priscilla in their dealings with Apollos (Acts 18:26). Who can tell what exciting opportunities may open up to us? We are called to preach everywhere, and God Himself has promised to work with us, confirming the word with signs following. (See Mark 16:20; Matthew 28:19-20.)

Saved by a Servant

In II Kings chapter five the sacred pen drew a sharp contrast between two individuals. In the household of Naaman, captain of the host of the king of Syria, lived a servant girl from Israel. Naaman, "a great man" with the king, had gained acclaim by delivering Syria (probably from Assyria). Verse one says he was "a mighty man in valour." Of the young maiden we know very little beyond the fact that she had been taken captive by the Syrians and waited on Naaman's wife.

Naaman, with all his fame and prestige, had one problem that blighted all his hopes: he was a leper. Like the sinner who achieves success in this world, there was still something sapping the joy from his life. Leprosy, a loathsome disease and a type of sin in the Bible, had taken hold of Naaman. The mighty hero of Syria could not shake the unmistakable feeling that he was doomed.

God used the young maiden girl to direct Naaman to Israel's God. Faith comes by hearing, and at the right moment the girl told her mistress, "Would God my lord were with the prophet that is in Samaria! for he would recover him of his leprosy" (II Kings 5:3). Although he was a proud man, when Naaman heard of the girl's words he acted decisively. A simple testimony, uttered with conviction and compassion, shook the nobleman's household. Even the kings of Syria and Israel became involved. Naaman set out for Israel with a huge reward and, for the first time, a glimmer of true faith in his heart.

What if the servant girl had failed to do her part? What if she had let bitterness against the Syrians silence her testimony? Surely in that case, there would have been no meeting between Elisha and Naaman and no miraculous healing of the latter. As it was, Naaman became a believer in the one true

God. "Behold, now I know," he declared, "that there is no God in all the earth, but in Israel" (II Kings 5:15).

Young people on fire for God have a unique testimony. Today the world seems to expect the worst of youth. It is surprising, even startling, for many to see the exact opposite of rebellion in this age group. The teenager or young adult who lives a clean, wholesome life and speaks unashamedly for his Lord is a powerful force. He will shake his world around him.

When a young person stands out boldly for the Lord it does something for him as well as for others. His commitment to Christ deepens, and his values are arranged in proper order.

Not to acknowledge Christ is to deny Him. Jesus Himself said, "Whosoever therefore shall confess me before men, him will I confess also before my Father which is in heaven. But whosoever shall deny me before men, him will I also deny before my Father which is in heaven" (Matthew 10:32-33).

Why Young People Fail To Witness

Witnessing is a work of the Spirit. Jesus said, "For without me ye can do nothing" (John 15:5). The natural man cringes at the thought of openly confessing the Lord. "I don't want to be a Jesus freak," or "I'll be a silent witness" may be our excuse, but there is a weakness in a Christian who fails to share his testimony. If we care we must share.

The greatest hindrance in witnessing for Jesus Christ is our pride. We think too much of ourselves and too little of our Lord. Certainly there is a reproach associated with the gospel. We get our English word *stigmatize* from the Greek *stigma,* which literally meant a brand or mark either tattooed or burnt on the body.

Paul the apostle wrote in Galatians 6:17, "From henceforth let no man trouble me: for I bear in my body the marks of the Lord Jesus." Most probably the apostle was referring to the scars on his body, the grim reminders of the persecution he had received for preaching Christ. Criminals and slaves in that day were often branded in reproach, but Paul bore his "marks" with honor. They were the tokens of his love for the gospel.

Does it seem strange that God would use a captive girl to witness to Naaman? Not so! Prisoners and slaves are a peculiar lot. You may strip them of much of their natural pride, but you cannot always crush their spirit. Their ardor flames brightest under difficulty. Prison chains only fanned the flame of Paul's love for Christ. He fully understood that because of the gospel his life was being forfeited. "For the which cause I also suffer these things: nevertheless I am not ashamed: for I know whom I have believed" (II Timothy 1:12).

If we are ashamed of Christ, perhaps we need more than an occasional trip to the altar and more than a few tears of emotion. It seems all too easy for us to forget the promises which we have made at youth camps or youth conventions. All our commitments need to be costly commitments, and all our promises need to be faithfully kept.

Methods or Motives?

In the winning of souls young people sometimes look for new methods. Impatient, they feel that if only the right scheme were devised then the church would be flooded with newcomers. The church, they believe, would soon have to be enlarged or a new building lot would have to be purchased.

The truth lies not so much in our methods but more in our motives. If we are motivated by the Holy

Ghost, we will be witnesses of God's power (Acts 1:8).

After reading about Paul's difficulties, (II Corinthians 4:8-10; 11:23-28) we might wonder what kept him preaching the gospel. Paul himself answered the question when he stated, "For the love of Christ constraineth us; because we thus judge, that if one died for all, then were all dead" (II Corinthians 5:14).

If we really believe that a person is drowning, and if we really care, then we will do anything to save him. We may first look for a boat, and if there is no boat, we may look for a life preserver. Without boat, life preserver, rope or pole, we are likely to take to the water ourselves.

Paul explained that he reached for those under the law (the Jews) and those outside the law (the Gentiles). "I have [in short] become all things to all men, that I might by all means—at all costs and in any and every way—save some [by winning them to faith in Jesus Christ]" (I Corinthians 9:22, *The Amplified Bible*).

Every godly method may be used effectively to win souls. What will work with one person may not work with another. Some individuals are readers and may be stimulated by means of tracts or books. Others, with little time or interest for reading, may enjoy taped music and preaching. Still others may enjoy the relaxed atmosphere of a home Bible study.

Our job is to keep fishing. If the fish are not taking worms, the wise angler will change to flies. "He that winneth souls is wise" (Proverbs 11:30).

To explain what it means to love our neighbor, Jesus told the story of the good Samaritan. Two very religious persons, a priest and a Levite, passed by on the other side of the road when they saw the half-dead Jew. What was it that caused the Samaritan to stop, even at great expense and danger to himself? "When he saw him, he had compassion on him" (Luke 10:33).

Jesus was moved with compassion when He saw the multitudes. Those who are filled with the Spirit of Christ will feel that same deep concern for souls. If we have lost our burden, then repentance, coupled with prayer and fasting, will renew our concern.

The Power of Our Witness

Two young men worked side by side in a factory. Their backgrounds were different and so were their viewpoints on life. The older of the two worked in the factory on a permanent basis. Though he had never finished high school, this individual had received the baptism of the Holy Ghost and was active as a youth leader in a Pentecostal church.

The younger man was simply earning money during the summer to help pay university expenses. He, too, had been religious, but he was actually offended by the presence of this "holy roller." The Pentecostal easily might have said too much or said nothing at all. Instead he simply stated, "Isn't God good?" Those three words brought deep conviction to the younger man's heart. Years later, after graduation from the university, he also was baptized in the name of Jesus Christ and received the Holy Ghost.

Again, the greatest obstacle to a person's being saved is his pride. A person would be willing to sacrifice time and money in religious pursuits, if he could do it on his terms. But the gospel strikes a devastating blow to all our haughty conceit. Generally a sinner, though he is down and out, will build some kind of barrier in his mind against God's plan of redemption. The woman at the well tried to hide behind a religious argument when Jesus met her. This was true, despite the fact that she was living in adultery.

Poor Naaman, plagued by leprosy, almost missed

his healing. He had expected some great fanfare and ceremony when he came to Elisha's house. Instead, Elisha's message, delivered by his servant, instructed the Syrian general to wash in the Jordan River seven times.

The prophet's words in their simplicity had offended Naaman, but not his servants. It was these servants' advice that saved the day. With great love and respect they addressed Naaman, "My father, if the prophet had bid thee do some great thing, wouldest thou not have done it? how much rather then, when he saith to thee, Wash, and be clean?" (II Kings 5:13).

Oh, the power of the spoken word! The servants, knowing their master would have paid any price to obtain healing, counseled him to receive that which would cost him nothing.

Prayer and Patience

Only the church can give birth to new souls. Conception takes place when the seed of the Word is sown in the sinner's heart (I Peter 1:23). An anointed testimony has power in itself to begin the process of spiritual life, but even at that, the work of the soulwinner is far from complete. Sometimes it takes months, even years, to see a convert grow into maturity in Christ.

Usually there is some struggle and strain after the new birth by water and Spirit. The new convert is especially susceptible to criticism. He is sensitive to his own failures. He may well be thrown off balance by false doctrine or by his own changing emotions. No wonder Paul addressed some of his converts as, "My little children, of whom I travail in birth again until Christ be formed in you" (Galatians 4:19).

Infant mortality is high when too little care is taken of the newborn. Often converts have to be taught the rudiments of living for God. They may not know how to pray or praise. Their knowledge of the Bible may be limited. But just as newborn children in the natural do those things which are necessary, so Christian babes, given the right circumstances, should grow in grace.

Much prayer and patience are needed if a person is to be an effective worker for the Lord. His vision of God's power must never dim. It is so easy to become discouraged. It is so easy to give up on an individual before God gives up. As long as the Holy Ghost is moving on the soul, and as long as that person honestly desires the Lord, there is hope. The Lord is "not willing that any should perish, but that all should come to repentance" (II Peter 3:9).

As with all education, the convert will learn best by observation and participation. If we first win his confidence and respect, he will use us as a role model. His prayers will be as earnest at the altar as are ours; his faith may rise or fall with our faith.

There is an amusing yet sobering correspondence between the actions of new converts and those they admire. Our response to worship may well become the response of another—be it a careless indifference or sincere, heart-felt worship. A Christian's attitude towards authority is most important since new converts will probably follow his example.

Who Will Reach Them?

Enthusiasm and youthfulness seem to go together. Although many teenagers and people in their twenties seem intent on burning themselves out on drugs and alcohol, there are many others who are reaching for real goals in life. They are looking for reality.

Someone or something will reach our generation. Political, military and religious leaders are keenly aware that the youth of any movement will largely determine its success or its failure. Dashing uniforms and colorful banners did much to convert German school children to Nazism in the 1930s. With thousands of teenagers shouting "Heil Hitler!" the Fuhrer propelled himself forward on his mad mission of conquest.

The brimming vitality and strength of youth is needed in the work of the gospel. The Apostle John declared, "I have written unto you, young men, because ye are strong, and the word of God abideth in you, and ye have overcome the wicked one" (I John 2:14).

Young people have physical strength to fast and to pray for revival. They should also have the spiritual stamina to lead in worship and to pray seekers through to the Holy Ghost.

If the younger generation is to be reached it will be reached by those within its own ranks. Courage is caught as well as taught. Young people still admire those who stand up for their convictions.

Create Our Own Atmosphere

Christians are involved in the greatest challenge of all the ages. Those to whom we witness must see a boldness in our lives. They must know that we are unashamedly giving our best to Jesus Christ. There can be no shame or sham in our testimony. We need to ask God to help us overcome any fear and hesitancy. "Ye are the light of the world. A city that is set on an hill cannot be hid" (Matthew 5:14).

The sinner needs to know that the most exciting thing he could possibly do is to serve God. By our witness we can help him realize that Jesus is very much alive. Everything we say to him about church and salvation should be positive and thrilling. There is an old adage that says, "Though you lead a horse to water, you cannot make him drink." That may be so, but a few trips to the salt block and the horse will get extremely thirsty. Jesus said, "Ye are the salt of the earth" (Matthew 5:13).

When the unsaved person comes to church at our invitation, he should be expecting something unusual to happen. We should already have told him that the Holy Ghost moves in the services. It should be no surprise to the newcomer when people express great joy and speak in tongues. After all, he has come expecting something different from what he has been accustomed to. Our church is different. We have told him so.

Many sinners in the early days of the Pentecostal movement of this century came to church because they considered it the nearest thing to a circus. They found, however, far more than a show, and many were saved.

Christians can help provide the atmosphere for our special guest. When he comes to church he should be introduced to the pastor. We should provide him with a song book and sit next to him. We should sing and worship with all our hearts and pray silently that God will speak to our friend's heart, and when he does respond, we can encourage him. We are living in the last days, and many do receive the Holy Ghost on their first trip to a Pentecostal altar.

Those who receive the Holy Ghost need our help. They may not understand what they have received. They will certainly need instruction in the Word of God. We should call them on the telephone and make sure that they have transportation to and from church.

Discipling is very important. According to the New Testament, Jesus actually seemed to have spent more time instructing the twelve than He did in witnessing to the lost. Paul the apostle was particularly concerned that other workers should be trained in practical matters of the church. (See

I Timothy, II Timothy and Titus.) The time we spend in discipling is well spent. "The things that thou hast heard of me among many witnesses," Paul wrote, "the same commit thou to faithful men, who shall be able to teach others also" (II Timothy 2:2).

Is It Too Late?

We are quickly running out of time. Our generation will never hear the gospel as it should be heard unless young Christians catch the vision.

Millions of single people, as well as young marrieds, are devoted to the cult of pleasure and worship at the altar of sensuality. In the United States the Public Health Service has estimated, for example, that one million illegal abortions are performed annually. Wild weekend parties and weekend sporting events overshadow church attendance. The pulsating beat of heavy rock music has saturated our society. Too often the normal seems to be the abnormal. Few people feel restrained. "Just get in the fast lane and stay there," seems to be the thinking of the day.

Is it too late? Is it too late for us to present the gospel to a dying world?

It is too late only if we think so. The great commission of Jesus Christ has never been rescinded. The command stands firm, "Go ye into all the world, and preach the gospel to every creature. He that believeth and is baptized shall be saved" (Mark 16:15-16).

The message of salvation still works. The lives of drug addicts, homosexuals, thieves and sinners of every description can be, and are being, changed. God is raising up a generation of faithful witnesses. They relate to this generation because many of them have been delivered by the power of the gospel.

Test Your Knowledge

Give the Scripture references:
1. _____ "And they went forth, and preached everywhere, the Lord working with them, and confirming the word with signs following. Amen."
2. _____ "Would God my lord were with the prophet that is in Samaria!"
3. _____ "But whosoever shall deny me before men, him will I also deny before my Father which is in heaven."
4. _____ "From henceforth let no man trouble me: for I bear in my body the marks of the Lord Jesus."
5. _____ "Ye are the light of the world. A city that is set on an hill cannot be hid."

Apply Your Knowledge

Consider ways in which you can witness for the Lord. Often opportunities will present themselves when we are talking to people individually. Showing interest in and consideration for others is critical. We possibly witness best when we meet others on their level. Jesus began His testimony to the woman at the well by asking her for some water.

Expand Your Knowledge

Young people have often been accused of worshiping rock stars, movie stars, or sports celebrities. In the next chapter you will be considering the matter of "true worship." Read John 4:21-24 to see what Jesus said on this subject.

8 Youth and Worship

Let every thing that hath breath praise the LORD. Praise ye the LORD.

Psalm 150:6

Start With the Scriptures

II Samuel 6:12-15 Romans 12:1
Psalm 47:1-2; 95; 149; 150 Ephesians 5:19
Acts 1:14; 2:1-4; 16:22-40 I Thessalonians 5:18
I Timothy 2:8

Everyone worships something. Worship is an expression from the heart of deep admiration and appreciation. Men worship peers; they worship wives; they worship respectable teachers. Worship is actually something that comes natural to man. He does not have to learn how to do it; he just does it.

Outward expressions of that heart-felt worship vary from person to person. One's personality causes him to express himself in his own peculiar way, and that expression may turn out quite different from those around him. But when it comes to worship given to God, the Bible has displayed what is acceptable to God. Men do not have to be in doubt as to what action to take to properly express their gratitude and admiration to God.

Honest men will admit to a deep-seated urge to recognize God in some way. They want to be sure that the way they recognize God is acceptable to Him. David prayed honestly, "Let the words of my mouth, and the meditation of my heart, be acceptable in thy sight, O LORD" (Psalm 19:14). And the Bible has made it plain for every honest inquirer of truth today to know how to worship God in ways that are acceptable to Him.

We will study those verses that illuminate worship in three basic areas: the physical act of worship; the mental attitude of worship; and the spiritual aspect of worship.

The Physical Act of Worship

The body is involved in worship. "I beseech you therefore, brethren, by the mercies of God, that ye present your bodies a living sacrifice, holy, acceptable unto God, which is your reasonable service" (Romans 12:1). While it is undeniable that this word from Paul is admonishing us toward personal holiness, it is also true that this word is showing us a physical service which is acceptable unto God.

If that was the only verse indicating that physical involvement was acceptable to God we might not make a case of it. But it is not the only verse. In fact, there are many.

Clapping hands is acceptable worship. The psalmist David admonished, "O clap your hands, all ye people" (Psalm 47:1), and they were not being instructed to make the physical effort of clapping the hands just for a rousing noise, but in order to worship. "The LORD most high is terrible; he is a great King over all the earth" (Psalm 47:2). The clapping of hands is not only an acceptable form of worship for the Lord, it is an important form.

Lifting our hands in honor to God is an acceptable form of worship to God. "Thus will I bless thee while I live," wrote David when he was in the wilderness of Judah. "I will lift up my hands in thy name" (Psalm 63:4). "Thus will I bless thee," wrote David. To bless the Lord is to worship Him.

Apparently this practice was still common by the time the church was well established, and equally apparent is the fact that God was still pleased with it as a form of worship to Him. God inspired Paul to write: "I will therefore that men pray every where, lifting up holy hands" (I Timothy 2:8).

Lifting one's voice, praying out loud, is acceptable physical worship to God. It is still heard now and then that someone complains about group praying, that is, the kind of praying where everyone prays out loud all at once. It is confusing, they say, and therefore unacceptable as a church practice.

The question must be asked: Confusing to whom? If the answer is that it is confusing to men, the rebuttal must be that prayers and worship are not offered for men's ears anyway, but for God's. If a person thought that it confused God to hear all men pray out loud and at the same time, his faith would be in an awfully small God.

David spoke for himself when he said, "As for me, I will call upon God; and the LORD shall save me. Evening, and morning, and at noon, will I pray, and cry aloud: and he shall hear my voice" (Psalm 55:16-17). The psalmist spoke for the whole church prophetically when he wrote, "and her saints shall shout aloud for joy" (Psalm 132:16).

Certainly we understand that all things should be done "decently and in order" (I Corinthians 14:40).

If an entire church service consisted of everyone talking at the same time the result would be confusion. But in the special times within the order of a church service when everyone is asked to pray, the scriptural order is still to pray aloud. At such times it is not only appropriate for all to pray aloud, it is acceptable unto God.

The act of singing songs is acceptable as worship to God. "O come, let us sing unto the LORD: let us make a joyful noise to the rock of our salvation. Let us come before his presence with thanksgiving, and make a joyful noise unto him with psalms" (Psalm 95:1-2).

Paul believed the act of singing emanated from the heart. It is not just the making of melody for no purpose, but to express worship. However, some formalists have bent Paul's words until they have been used in contrast to what he must have actually meant. Paul said, "Speaking to yourselves in psalms and hymns and spiritual songs, singing and making melody in your heart to the Lord" (Ephesians 5:19). The formalists have emphasized the word *yourselves*. They would have us believe that Paul was giving us instructions here on how to conduct a church service. Truthfully, Paul was speaking to the Ephesians about their personal conduct, not their church services.

By the time the formalists get through with this verse, it reads something like this: "Be very quiet in church services because the only song you are supposed to sing is a silent one in your heart." But that is not what Paul said, and it is not what the verse means. Since "out of the abundance of the heart the mouth speaketh" (Matthew 12:34), Paul simply stated that if we put a song in our hearts, a song will come out.

Sometimes dancing is acceptable worship. Of course, David again becomes our teacher for what is acceptable in the way of worship. David the king was having the Ark of the Covenant brought into the city of David, and he preceded the procession "leaping and dancing before the LORD" (II Samuel 6:16). It is interesting to note that his wife, Michal, despised his dancing, chided him for it, and apparently gained the displeasure of God, never bearing children again as long as she lived (II Samuel 6:23).

David seemed not to have enjoyed this dance before the Lord as a one time thing, but instead encouraged all of God's people to so worship: "Let them praise his name in the dance" (Psalm 149:3). "Praise him with the timbrel and dance" (Psalm 150:4).

The question of governing usually arises on this topic: Who is in control, the person dancing, or the Lord? In other words, does a person stand and wait until God "moves" him to dance, or does he dance of his own voluntary will? David's dance was one of joy. It was his willful act. It was a voluntary expression. He just wanted to do it. And he did it "with all his might" (II Samuel 6:14).

It seems that all acts of worship must be the voluntary act on the part of the one doing the worshiping. To wait on God to move us is like someone not offering thanks to another unless he comes over and says, "Will you please tell me 'thank you?' " We praise God of our own choice. We worship Him because we want to, and we choose to do it.

There is a difference in action and reaction. My worship of God must be an action of my own choice. He simply deserves to be worshiped; therefore, I will worship Him in the ways He has shown me are acceptable to Him.

The Mental Attitude of Worship

It is possible for a person to go through all the

right motions of worship, to perform all the right deeds mentioned in the first part of this chapter, and still not be worshiping in a manner acceptable to God. God has given us the means whereby to worship Him, but He wants our worship to be much more than the performance of a few rituals. He wants it to come from our hearts.

There must be a genuine thankfulness in our worship. We are not to be actors, playing out a role on Sunday. We are to be thankful for all of God's blessings and therefore worship Him because we are. "In every thing give thanks: for this is the will of God in Christ Jesus concerning you" (I Thessalonians 5:18).

There must be a knowledge of truth in our worship. Does God accept worship that comes from one who is ignorant of His doctrines? Probably not. Jesus admitted that the Pharisees and the scribes worshiped Him, but of their worship He said: "But in vain do they worship me, teaching for doctrines the commandments of men" (Matthew 15:9). In other words, because they were teaching improper doctrines, their worship was in vain; it was not accepted.

Jesus also said that the time had come in which "true worshippers shall worship the Father in spirit and in truth: for the Father seeketh such to worship him. God is a Spirit: and they that worship him must worship him in spirit and in truth" (John 4:23-24). It seems from statements like these that God wants more than just the physical acts of worship. He requires a knowledge from the worshiper—the knowledge of truth. Worship which comes from someone who does not possess that knowledge may be in vain.

There must be an obedience to truth for our worship to be acceptable to God. Jesus startled His hearers with the statement: "Not every one that saith unto me, Lord, Lord, shall enter into the kingdom of heaven; but he that doeth the will of my

Father which is in heaven" (Matthew 7:21). "Lord, Lord" is a reference to prayer and worship, so Jesus is plainly saying that some people who have worshiped Him will not be saved. Why? It is because they did not do the will of the Father or obey Him.

The Spiritual Aspect

Now let us consider the spiritual aspect of worship. While worship is a voluntary outward expression of our gratitude and admiration of God, there are some spiritual values reaped by those who do worship.

Group worship brings a sense of God's presence to those who worship. We read that "where two or three are gathered together" there is God in the midst of them (Matthew 18:20). Now, we know that God is already in us when we gather, so what is the distinction in this coming together that causes God to speak as if He is in our midst in a special way, different somehow from the manner in which He always resides within us anyway?

The difference is this: the rest of the passage says that it is where two or three are gathered together in the name of Jesus that God manifests Himself in a special way. People coming together "in His name" suggests a common gathering of worshipers. Therefore we properly infer that when we gather to worship Jesus, He comes into our midst in a dimension other than the one in which He already resides. It is an especially meaningful presence of the Lord.

Is there anything significant in the fact that Christ identifies Himself somehow more fully in the company of "two or three"? Of course there is. We may properly describe a typical church service as the place where "two or three" come together, and we may further assume that there is something special about God's presence at such a gathering that one may not witness in his own private devotions.

Some argue today that since God is everywhere, and since He lives within us, we do not have to feel obligated to attend church services. Some carry the argument further and suggest that watching a televised church service, or listening to audio tapes of services, carries the same influence as being present, but this is not so. The Bible clearly teaches that something special regarding God's visitation occurs where "two or three" come together in the name of Jesus.

It may also be said that no command of the Scriptures is given without good cause. When God tells us to do something, there is a good reason for it. We may not always understand the reason, but it exists. Therefore, since the Bible teaches us to "not forsake" the assembling together with one another (Hebrews 10:25), we may assume that God has a good reason for us to do so. And we may further assume that it is because He wants to visit us in a special way, a way He has made possible only through group gatherings for worship.

However, it must not be overlooked that personal and private worship of God brings a sense of God's presence nearer to the worshiper. We all have God's presence in our hearts if we have been filled with His Spirit. Private worship enhances the sense of God's nearness to the individual. Group worship with "two or three" further enhances the awareness of His presence, and that allows God the space to perform miracles or do special works that are needed in His body of believers.

Regarding the benefits of worship, one of the most enlightening verses may be Psalm 22:3: "But thou art holy, O thou that inhabitest the praises of Israel." The verb *inhabitest* connotes dwelling, or pitching one's tent, and the implication is plain: when anyone praises God, He comes to dwell, to "pitch His tent" and stay awhile, in that person's presence. What an incentive to magnify and worship God in the manner which He finds acceptable!

The arrangement of the tribes around the wilderness Tabernacle teaches us that entrance into the presence of the Most High is accomplished only through praise and worship. The tribes were specifically placed by God, and He designated the tribe of Judah to be placed on the eastmost side, the side where was the only entrance into the Tabernacle, and hence into the Holy of Holies.

The implication should not be lost on us. If we would enter into the "Holy of Holies," if we would know God in the most intimate of relationships, we will do so only by passing through "praise." By the arrangement of the tribe of Judah, every Israelite who entered the Tabernacle would have passed through "praise," for the name *Judah* means "praise." Did not David tell Israel to "enter into His gates with thanksgiving, and into His courts with praise"? (Psalm 100:4).

Worship has a liberating quality about it. We enjoy reading the fascinating account of Paul and Silas being cast into the "inner prison." They, having their feet made fast in stocks, could still find something to rejoice over, for at midnight they "sang praises unto God" (Acts 16:25). The foundation of the prison was disturbed by an earthquake, the doors were all thrown open and the prisoners loosed. While we are not told in the Scriptures that it occurred as a direct result of their worship, it certainly seems probable by the fact that the Bible links the two events in adjoining verses.

Men often find themselves in "prisons" in life. They are tending to the things of God, minding their own business, and the enemy comes to them and binds them in harsh circumstancial prisons. Let the

Christian who finds himself in such a predicament take heart. There is an escape from the mental and spiritual prisons—worship!

There is sometimes a span of time between the moment one professes his belief in Jesus Christ and the coming of Christ into his heart in the form of the Holy Spirit. What is one to do during that span of time? When a person repents of his sins, is baptized in Jesus' name, and asks the Lord to fill him with the Holy Spirit, if that filling does not come to him immediately, what is he to do? He should worship God. And in his worshiping, God will come to him.

It is worthy of note that Jesus sent His faithful followers back to Jerusalem to "wait" for the promise to come. What were they to do while they were "waiting"? Acts chapters one and two tell the story. They continued in prayer and supplication, and then the Holy Ghost fell on them all. (See also Luke 24:53.) Let the man who finds himself "waiting" today continue in prayer and worship, and the Holy Ghost will come to him also.

Test Your Knowledge

True or False

_____ 1. Worship comes naturally to mankind.

_____ 2. The Bible has explained what kinds of physical acts God accepts as worship.

_____ 3. The body, or physical action, is not necessary in worshiping God.

_____ 4. God accepts worship, even if it comes from one who teaches false doctrine.

_____ 5. Worship brings the presence of God nearer.

Fill in the blanks:

6. The body is useful in worshiping God; He is worshiped by _____ hands, by _____ one's voice in prayer, by _____ songs, and

in other ways as well.

7. The name Judah means _____, and the tribe of Judah was situated on the _____ side of the Tabernacle.

8. "But thou art holy, O thou that _____ the praises of Israel."

9. Paul and Silas worshiped and found that _____ doors are opened thereby.

10. A man "waiting" for the Holy Ghost to come should _____.

Apply Your Knowledge

The best way to discover the benefits of worship is to practice worshiping. Set aside two minutes in the morning (anyone can spare two minutes) for the sole purpose of praising and glorifying God. Do not ask for anything from Him. Do not name needs and problems. Simply worship Him. Find new expressions to tell Him how much He means to you. Then, during the day find opportunities to breathe short prayers of praise. Within a week you should begin to experience a sense of God being closer to you, and your "prison doors" should begin to open.

Expand Your Knowledge

With a concordance look up the word *praise* and similar words only in the Book of Psalms. Single out two or three Psalms for complete analysis. Discover how much worship was a part of David's life and see if you can understand why God would have labeled David a man after His own heart. Make honest attempts to incorporate the kind of praise you discover in your study of the Psalms into your own experience.

Youth and Availability

9

Whatsoever thy hand findeth to do, do it with thy might; for there is no work, nor device, nor knowledge, nor wisdom, in the grave, whither thou goest.

Ecclesiastes 9:10

Start With the Scriptures

Isaiah 6:8
Ezekiel 22:30
Matthew 4:19-22
Luke 22:33
John 6:1-9
II Corinthians 8:5

What talent would a person choose as the most valuable talent anyone could possess in the church? If we were asked to name the one talent we thought to be the most valuable, what would we name?

Singing? Who can deny the value of singing to the part of a church service devoted to worship?

Music? Who can imagine being without the music in church services? What a wonderful atmosphere is created by properly played music, designed to aid in the worship of God.

Soulwinning? If there were no soulwinners in the church, the church would soon cease to exist, there being no new members to replace the old.

Preaching? Obviously preaching is the heart of every service at our churches, for it is through the foolishness of preaching that God chose to save them that believe.

Administration? Some churches suffer, not for lack of good preaching and singing, but for lack of sound administration. No one who is knowledgeable about church government would deny the importance of administrative talents.

Would we name the mechanical talents, such as electrical repair, plumbing repair, electronics repairs, construction skills, and others? Obviously, we owe much to the skills of those in our churches who have saved us countless thousands of labor dollars because they gave their skill or talent to the work of the church.

But suppose we were told that none of those talents is the most valuable talent in the church? Would we be surprised? Well, it is the truth. None of those talents, as valuable as they are, even approaches being the most valuable.

The Most Wonderful Talent in the Church

The most useful and important talent in the church is one that:
- Is not inherited, but acquired;
- Cannot be bought with money, so anyone, regardless of his financial capabilities, can acquire it;
- Age has no bearing on, for sometimes the younger members of a church are more likely to possess it than older ones are.

The most wonderful talent is *availability*. Of what value is it to a church to have the finest pianist in the land if he is never available to play? What does it matter if a church has a member with tremendous soulwinning skills, if he is always working too much to put them to use? He is not available.

Who cares if there is a lady with a beautiful voice, one who could have sung "professionally" had she chosen, if she is not available to sing? Some churches have skilled craftsmen who could rebuild or repair any item in the building, yet doors hang loose, wallpaper peels off, roofs leak, and rest rooms wear permanent "out of order" signs. Although the craftsmen possess some wonderful talents, they do not necessarily possess the most wonderful talent—availability. Their abilities are worthless if they never have the time to put their skills to work.

The One Talent Found in All Great Men

Of all the great men and women in the world and in the church, talents and skills too numerous to mention have been considered to be their "strong points." Yet there is only one talent which they all have shared in common—availability.

Regardless of how many their other skills, and regardless of how proficient they were at them, had they not possessed this talent called availability their other skills would never have been recognized.

The Talent That Transcends Dispensational Eras

This talent is not new. It is not a "modern" idea. It is as old as mankind. Gideon employed it. Moses, who did not think he had the talent necessary to lead Israel, put this talent into action. Jonah developed this talent in the belly of a fish. He did not have it at first, but after a few hours in a fish's belly, he acquired it and once his feet hit the shore he was "available."

New Testament era preachers were still discovering its value. Twelve disciples had it. When Jesus interviewed candidates for the leadership of His new era, He did not thrust a credit report under their noses to see if they were financially sound. Nor did He hand them a "Talent Survey" form to find out if they had useful skills for His work. He did not inquire into their backgrounds to be sure they were born on the "right side of the tracks." He did not check to see if they had been educated in the proper schools of the day so that they would represent Him well.

There seems, in fact, to have been only one real qualification He was looking for. As He walked by them, He said: "Follow Me!" And if they possessed this wonderful talent, they arose (for they had time and were available) and followed Him. When He found men with that qualification, He was pleased to make them His own. He seemed to know that He could train them in whatever other skills they might need in His service, as long as they were available.

It is still the same today as it has been over thousands of years. The best talent is availability.

Some Great Men Who Were Available

History will tell us that Martin Luther King, Jr., was a great orator, a great tactician, and a great social reformer. Perhaps he possessed other valuable skills as well. But history books will probably miss his greatest talent—he was available.

He was pastoring a small church called Dexter Avenue Baptist Church. He was like any other black pastor in the rural south. He tended to his church business. He preached his Sunday sermons. And he hoped that he would be able to continue doing so without government intervention or persecution, for those were stormy days for blacks.

Rosa Parks was a little black seamstress, tired from a day's work, who boarded a city bus in Montgomery, Alabama, and took the only open seat. It happened to be situated near the front, and that was for "whites only." A white man boarded, and seeing her sitting in that section demanded that she move to the rear, even though she would have to stand there. But she was tired, physically and emotionally, and she refused. The bus driver would not move the bus, and Rosa would not move from her seat. The police were called and Rosa was arrested.

Some of the black leaders became alarmed. A few ministers got together and decided to take some course of action. Someone suggested a boycott of the bus services. But no one felt that he knew what to do.

One of the ministers in that little circle thought of the pastor of Dexter Avenue Baptist Church. He knew him to be energetic and diplomatic. Perhaps, he thought, he could offer some real direction. So he went to his phone and dialed. When he explained the situation to Martin Luther King, Jr., he concluded his appeal with one question: "Will you help?"

History records his achievements, but his achievements would never have come about if he had answered that question wrongly. If he had said, "I'd like to, but I don't have time," or, "Sounds good, but I'm not your man," we would probably never have heard of the man. But because he possessed the most wonderful talent, history has been forever changed. He was available.

We all know of Paul's missionary journeys. No one dismisses the impact his ministry has had on the church. We have repeated the story of his life in many Sunday school classes and sermons. We can probably list the number of beatings he received, recall his shipwrecks and quote many of his sayings. But in our rightful recognition of his greatness, let us not overlook the fact that none of those experiences would ever have occurred if Paul had not possessed the most wonderful talent in the church—availability.

He never lost his talent. When he intended to go to Bithynia, he had a vision of a man saying, "Come on over to Macedonia and help us." And the Bible tells us that he "immediately" went. He could have thought of a thousand reasons not to go. He could have at least taken several days to prepare. But he had the talent; he was available.

We love to read of Elisha's exploits and to think that he had a "double portion" of that spirit that Elijah, his predecessor, had. We marvel at his confidence and faith. Yet we might never have read of Elisha if he also had not possessed the talent of which we speak. When Elijah saw Elisha, the latter was plowing in a field. Elijah walked past him, flinging his mantle upon Elisha's shoulders as he walked by. With no more of an introduction than that, Elisha "left the oxen, and ran after Elijah," saying, "I will follow thee" (I Kings 19:20). He was available.

Great Young Men Who Had the Talent

Age is no factor in possessing this wonderful talent, and there are a couple of prime examples to that end in the Bible.

David was a young shepherd when he visited the army of Israel to bring his brothers a little something from home and to pick up some news to carry back to his father. While he was in the camp, he witnessed the boasting of Goliath, taunting the Israelite soldiers. Amazingly to David, no one took up the challenge Goliath issued. David was not a soldier; he was a shepherd. David was not big enough to wear the soldier's armor. They fitted him with some and he could not wear it. But what he lacked in some talents he made up in his availability. Perhaps we could have read about some other young man, a soldier, in the Bible's account of Goliath's demise, but no one else was available; only David offered himself.

There is a remarkable story in the New Testament about the feeding of five thousand. The crowd had followed Jesus up into a mountainous area. It was late, and He saw that they might faint by the way without food, and so He asked for food. A young boy had five loaves and two fish. He had something else, too. He had the talent that is so wonderful. He made his little lunch available.

The Only Talent God Really Needs

The aforementioned characters teach us something else about the work of God. Too often we are guilty of admiring men because of what we perceive their worth to the kingdom of God to be. "Oh," we say, "won't her voice be a blessing to the church?" Or possibly we see a wealthy member added to the church roll and we think, "He will surely be a blessing to the church." Yet, if voices and money are never made available, of what value are they?

One pastor told of an interesting experience which occurred in his church. An elderly lady had repeatedly gone to his music director and asked if she might be put on the list to sing solos on Sunday nights. "Are you a competent singer?" asked the director of music. "I just do my best for the Lord," was her simple reply.

The director found ways to keep her name off the list after someone told him that she had stood beside the lady during congregational songs, and that she definitely was not "Sunday night material." However, the lady was insistent. Finally, conscience prevailed and the director told her to have a song ready, that he might just call on her on the spur of the moment. Secretly, he planned to wait until some mid-week service night when no visitors were present and give her space to sing her song. And that is what he did.

Those who were there when she warbled her tune would speak respectfully of that night. They would not be able to describe what it was they felt when she sung. They would offer some suggestions. Some said it was her sincerity. Others said it was her quiet tears. The pastor simply said that the Spirit took over at that moment, and he did not see that his sermon would improve upon the work.

What really happened is this. God saw a little woman with a tiny talent. Reminiscent of David and the little lad with a lunch, He chose to show that He is not limited to the "professional" talents of men. He took her meager abilities because they were available, and he multiplied them to meet the needs of hearts in that church meeting.

Overcoming Difficulties

A careful analysis of Ecclesiastes 9:10 reveals a wonderful truth about our talents. It begins with "Whatsoever. . . ." The verse of Scripture does not specify particular talents our hands might find to engage in. It does not involve itself in degrees of perfection regarding our talents. It says simply, "Whatsoever thy hand findeth to do, do it with thy might."

Preeminence is often asserted to one or two talents in a church, and yet so many talents are critical to the successful work of God. The truth is that the performance of one or two special skills is not as critical as that all men make available whatever little talents they possess.

Several years ago an old man joined a small rural

church. It was soon discovered by the other members that the old man could not read or write. His signature (which he had to study over long and hard) was illegible. He could not carry a tune though he sung loudly on the hymns he had committed to memory. But he was wise beyond formal education. When he drove up in the church parking lot, if he saw paint blistering on the eaves, within the week he was buying paint and scraping the eaves. And most of the time no one in the church was aware of his work.

When the gravel parking lot had several potholes in it, he bought a load of gravel out of his own small wages, tied a steel bar behind his car, and filled and smoothed the holes. When the grass was growing, he walked the entire church property behind his own push mower. No one would have considered the old man to have any useful talents. He could not sing; he played no instrument. The children sometimes chuckled when he testified, for even they had better grammar than he. In terms of what we often esteem highly in a church, he did not measure up. But what little he saw that he could do, he did with all his might. He brought his ability and made it available. He gave it willingly. He possessed the most wonderful talent in the church.

Do What You Can

At the feeding of the five thousand, Jesus did not ask, "What do you lack?" He asked instead, "What have ye?" And He is asking us today, "What do you have? What are you capable of doing?" Can we paint a wall, trim hedges, mow grass, vacuum floors, clean a bathroom, polish furniture, pass out tracts? What are we capable of doing?

When a person finds some things that he can do, he should eliminate any hindrances to doing them.

Here are the kind of hindrances that are common:
- "None of the other young people do anything like that around the church."
  So what? We are not looking to see what others are doing (or are not doing). We are looking to see what we are personally able to do.
- "The other kids will think I'm trying to butter someone up if they see me doing a job like that."

We are not trying to impress people. We are trying to acquire the most wonderful talent in the church. What difference does it make if our friends can perform tremendous things, but they never do? What value is our talent if we never use it? We should forget what others are doing and look at what we can do.

Do the Best We Can

If a person sings, he should sing his best. If he mows the church lawn, he should mow it the best he can. A Christian should not do a task halfheartedly. He should do whatever he does as well as possible.

Practice does make perfect. The first time we perform a service for our church, we may feel that we have done it inadequately. But the next time we do it, we will know better how it should be done, and we will improve as time goes on.

Do for Others To Be Blessed

Imagine how many Israelites owed thanks to David for slaying Goliath. He blessed all of Israel. In fact, it appears that his only motive was in preserving the sanctity of Israel (I Samuel 17:26). He was available to serve others.

At least five thousand owed gratitude to the young lad who made his lunch available. He could not have been thinking selfishly, else he would have denied that he had a lunch and kept it hidden. But he made it available, willing to give it up that others might benefit.

A man told of being made to pick berries when he was a boy. It fell his task to gather berries for his mother. He resented it. There were other things he would rather do. But one day, rather than stomping through the berry patch in his usual fashion, he got a brainstorm. He thought how fun it might be to surprise everyone at supper by having plenty of extra berries. Instead of he and his sister and brother fussing over who got the most, he would see to it that there were enough berries for all of them to have their fill.

Picking berries in that manner made the time pass a lot more quickly, he noticed. He also noticed how enjoyable mealtime was when everyone was laughing about their surprise at all the berries he picked. The boy learned a valuable lesson about life that day. Life is much more enjoyable when talents and skills are given to usefulness for others.

Availability is a lesson we should all learn. A Christian should not complain because he has been asked to do some tedious task. "Whatsoever thy hand findeth to do, do it with thy might" (Ecclesiastes 9:10). When we do it to bless someone else, the task will cease to be tedious. It will be a joy.

Test Your Knowledge

1. What is the most wonderful talent in the church? _____
2. Is there any single skill which is more important than all the others in a church? Yes No
3. List two men who exemplify the talent of availability. _____ _____
4. It is impossible for human skills to do the work of the church without God's intervention. T F

5. Jesus apparently looked for only one talent when He selected His disciples: availability   T   F

Apply Your Knowledge

On a sheet of paper, draw a vertical line down the center of the page. On the left hand side of the column write the heading at the top of the page: "Skills Which I Possess." On the right hand side of the line, write this heading: "Actual Times I Have Employed My Skills."

Then write the skills you actually possess. List honestly any talent you have, or name the kinds of things you can do—singing, playing an instrument, polishing furniture, taking out garbage, vacuuming carpets, cleaning windows, painting walls, artistic skills, repairing air conditioning units, repairing electrical wiring, and so on. What skills do you use around your house, or on your job? List these on the left.

Then, on the right, write the actual times you have used your skills at your church. You might keep a running journal of such things for a few months.

This chart will tell you at a glance if you possess the most wonderful talent. If the left hand column contains a number of entries, but the right hand column contains few, you might want to ask God to help you find ways to put your skills to better usefulness in your church.

Expand Your Knowledge

Study the lives of four great men in the Bible and discover for yourself how often their skills were actually put into use for God. See if you do not find a consistent factor in each of them. They may not have had a greater wisdom or knowledge over their peers, but they were certainly more available.

Youth and Expendability 10

> *For if thou altogether holdest thy peace at this time, then shall there enlargement and deliverance arise to the Jews from another place; but thou and thy father's house shall be destroyed: and who knoweth whether thou art come to the kingdom for such a time as this?*
>
> *Esther 4:14*

Start With the Scriptures

Exodus 32:32
Esther 4:1-17
Romans 9:3; 12:3
Philippians 1:20-21

Often the greatest challenges of our lives come at the most unexpected moments. Perhaps we have just enjoyed the invigorating experience of standing on some mountaintop of faith. The joys of knowing God and His blessings have thrilled us. Somehow everything seems to be right and in its proper place. We may even have thought that these pleasant circumstances are just what God has intended for us to enjoy forever. Although there have been difficulties in the past, we might begin to imagine that life, from now on, will be a continuous series of happy events.

Suddenly a storm of great intensity breaks upon us. The winds and the rain seem all the more cruel because they were so unexpected. We know in our hearts that we have loved God and have tried to obey Him. Indeed, the storms in our lives often seem to arise from the very fact that we are doing God's will. The disciples, caught in a mighty gale on the Sea of Galilee, had simply followed Christ's commands.

Let us admit to ourselves that we need the storms. It would be a shame for any of us to think we are uniquely favored by God. God is not our servant; He is our master. God is sovereign. He has every right to say, "Is it not lawful for me to do what I will with mine own?" (Matthew 20:15).

If we are born of God, we belong to God. (See I Corinthians 6:19.) He can send us where He will or keep us waiting. He may choose to deliver us from our afflictions or give us grace to go through them. Our calling is to serve our loving Master in sickness or in health, in life or in death (Romans 14:8).

In a word, we who belong to the Almighty are expendable.

A Star Is Born

Who would have thought that Esther would one day become queen of Persia? Although her name means "star," she was only an orphan girl, for as the Bible records, "she had neither father nor mother" (Esther 2:7). Her parents, like her cousin Mordecai who raised her, had probably been led as captives from Jerusalem under Nebuchadnezzar.

This would hardly seem the background for a queen, but God has His way of bringing His purposes to pass. We can see the hand of the Almighty working with perfect timing, despite the fact that no direct mention of God's name is to be found in the Book of Esther.

In the third year of his reign, King Ahasuerus (Xerxes) made a great feast for his followers in Shushan the palace. The wine flowed freely, and "on the seventh day, when the heart of the king was merry with wine" (Esther 1:10), the king commanded his seven chamberlains to bring Vashti the queen to his side.

Meanwhile Queen Vashti (her name means "beauty") was holding a feast for the women in the royal house. When word came to Vashti that her husband wished "to shew the people and princes her beauty" (Esther 1:11), she flatly refused.

If, as it seems, Vashti was maintaining her modesty by refusing the royal command, she is to be highly commended. To expose herself before the eyes of drunken revellers would certainly have been degrading, especially for an Oriental queen. She was evidently a woman of courage whom we have to respect.

The king, however, was terribly angered. On the advice of his wise men (who themselves feared a general rebellion of the Persian women in their homes), Vashti was put away and a new queen was sought out. The most attractive young women of the kingdom were brought to Shushan the palace. In the plan of God, Esther was included in the contest. Captivated by the genuine beauty of this young Jewish maiden, Ahasuerus selected her to be the next queen.

Esther's opinion of herself could easily have changed after her marriage to the king. After all, Ahasuerus was the most powerful king in all the earth. Many women have become proud over much less recognition.

It was then that the young queen's real character was tested. How often people stay true to God while they are left in the background, but when they are brought out into the glamour of the world, something often happens. Their humility begins to fade. They lose sight of their own limitations and their former dependence upon God.

The critical point is not in what we say but in our choice of action. The world is always beckoning young people to taste of its "dainties." Wrong decisions, however, can affect our testimony for a lifetime.

The Approaching Storm

Haman the Agagite was especially fitted to serve Satan's purposes. A man of superior abilities, he had been chosen as the chief prince under King Ahasuerus. His opinions had a powerful effect upon the Persian monarch, and with arrogant pride Haman sought ways to advance his own cause.

Because Mordecai, Esther's cousin, had refused to bow down in obeisance to Haman, he developed a cunning plan to destroy all the Jews in Persia. "There is a certain people," so he informed the king, "scattered abroad and dispersed among the people in all the provinces of thy kingdom; and their laws are diverse from all people; neither keep they the king's laws: therefore it is not for the king's profit to suffer them. If it please the king, let it be written that they may be destroyed: and I will pay ten thousand talents of silver to the hands of those that have the charge of the business, to bring it into the king's treasures" (Esther 3:8-9).

Ahasuerus must have believed that Haman was honestly trying to strengthen the empire. The king designated ten thousand talents for the plan. Moreover, he gave Haman his signet ring to seal any letters which were necessary. Exactly eleven months from the day that the royal command was dispatched by messengers to all the provinces, a terrible slaughter of the Jews was due to take place.

A stone thrown into a pool of water will send out one rippling wave of disturbance after another. The terrible news from Shushan must have likewise affected the Jews. At the center of the disturbance was Mordecai. He could be seen just outside the palace gates. His clothing was now sackcloth and ashes, and he was wailing in his grief.

Apparently Esther had not yet heard of the decree against the Jews. She simply felt a terrible alarm because of the strange actions of Mordecai. Fearing for her cousin's reputation, if not for his life, the queen sent a change of clothing to Mordecai, but it was refused. Hatach the servant was then sent by Esther to determine what the problem really was.

The message which Hatach brought back to Esther must have been a bombshell. Not only did Mordecai want the queen to know of the impending disaster, but he also demanded that she become personally involved. He charged her "that she should go in unto the king, to make supplication unto him, and to make request before him for her people" (Esther 4:8).

To Esther, Mordecai's command was frightening. All Persia knew that for anyone to approach the king in the inner court without being called meant death "except such to whom the king shall hold out the golden sceptre, that he may live," and as Esther continued to tell Hatach, "I have not been called to come in unto the king these thirty days" (Esther 4:11). Since Ahasuerus had dealt so cruelly with the beautiful Vashti on a whim, could Esther expect any better treatment?

There seemed, however, no other way out of this situation. As much as Esther might have wished it were otherwise, Mordecai informed her through Hatach that she was the hope of the Jews. "Think not with thyself that thou shalt escape in the king's house, more than all the Jews. For if thou altogether holdest thy peace at this time, then shall there enlargement and deliverance arise to the Jews from another place; but thou and thy father's house shall be destroyed: and who knoweth whether thou art come to the kingdom for such a time as this?"

Being the excellent counselor that he was, Mordecai did not merely warn Esther of the danger of disobedience. He went further than that. Mordecai pointed Esther to a divine purpose for her life. These were desperate hours and moments for them both (as a seventy-five foot gallows would soon prove), but reason did not give way to panic. Mordecai directed his cousin to a nobler cause than that of being a Persian queen.

Called to the Kingdom

There is a kingdom far greater than any which men have established. Indeed, the prophet Daniel spoke to Nebuchadnezzar of four great human kingdoms, all of which would crumble (Daniel 2). The stone which broke the image to pieces is the kingdom of Jesus Christ. "And in the days of these kings shall the God of heaven set up a kingdom, which shall never be destroyed" (Daniel 2:44).

Jesus Himself said, "My kingdom is not of this world: if my kingdom were of this world, then would my servants fight" (John 18:36).

On the Day of Pentecost the kingdom of God came into the hearts of men with a mighty manifestation. Jesus had said, "But ye shall receive power, after that the Holy Ghost is come upon you" (Acts 1:8). We bear the seal of the King of kings, and have authority, among other things, to cast out devils, to speak with new tongues and to lay hands on the sick that they may recover. (See Mark 16:17-18.) This is all reminiscent of that ancient day when King Ahasuerus asked, "What shall be done unto the man whom the king delighteth to honour?" (Esther 6:6). And the answer, though it came unwittingly from the lips of Haman, holds a great promise for every believer: "Let the royal apparel be brought which the king useth to wear, and the horse that the king rideth upon, and the crown royal which is set upon his head" (Esther 6:8).

Paul the apostle wrote, "If we suffer, we shall also reign with him" (II Timothy 2:12).

Surely, though we lose everything in this life, it is well worth the price to serve Christ. We should let the Lord set up His dominion in our hearts. "For the kingdom of God is not meat and drink; but righteousness, and peace, and joy in the Holy Ghost" (Romans 14:17).

For Such a Time as This

Some of the Jews in Persia may well have thought that they had reached their end. The pressure upon these people must have been terrific. They may well have felt like prisoners on death row, waiting for the day of execution. A holocaust certainly looked to be imminent.

The Jews were strangers in a foreign land and were viewed with suspicion by many of the Persians. More than that, Satan was intent on destroying God's chosen people to the last man, woman and child.

In the critical times in which we now live, it would be easy to despair. Young people, in particular, seem to be without any clear sense of direction. A host of them have acted on the mistaken idea, "If it feels good, do it." They have set sail on the raging seas of drug addiction, alcoholism or illicit sex, and to their own dismay, have found they were never quite the same afterward. A feeling of gloom or fatalism often followed them. Numbers have taken the ultimate step and committed suicide.

The world needs men like Mordecai who can give others a glimpse of the divine perspective. In that dark hour in Persia he still had hope that God's will was being done. The young queen, he believed, could be instrumental at that time in delivering her nation.

God's timing was so important. He who sees the end from the beginning was well aware of the situation. (See Isaiah 46:10.) His schedule would not be too late for all those still trusting in Him.

If I Perish, I Perish

Esther, in her modesty and purity, may well represent the church of the living God. Though she came from a humble background, this young maiden had an inner beauty which God highly valued. (See I Peter 3:4.) Already she had obeyed Mordecai's request not to reveal her nationality, and by her submissive spirit, Esther proved she could be trusted.

Be assured that there is a vital role for young people to fulfill in these last days. The younger generation is not just important to the cause of God; it is essential to the cause of God. When Goliath called for a man to fight at Shochoh, the experienced soldiers of Israel "were sore afraid" (I Samuel 17:24). Their fear crippled their faith, and so God had to use a shepherd boy. His elder brothers were actually angry at David for believing God, and King Saul doubtfully stated, "You are not able to go to fight against the Philistine. You are only an adolescent" (I Samuel 17:33, *The Amplified Bible*).

In the face of such discouraging circumstances many would have trembled, but David triumphed. Since God has never intended anything else except victory for His people, we need never fail.

The circumstances were certainly difficult for Esther as well. She knew the danger of obeying Mordecai, but her sense of commitment was greater than all her fears. Courageously she responded to her cousin, "Go, gather together all the Jews that are present in Shushan, and fast ye for me, and neither eat nor drink three days, night or day: I also and my maidens will fast likewise; and so will I go in unto the king, which is not according to the law: and if I perish, I perish" (Esther 4:16).

Here was the highest kind of commitment. When Esther walked out of the comparative safety of her palace apartment and into the king's inner court, she died to her self-interests. She was declaring that she was expendable. Her personal safety at that moment was far less important to her than the cause she represented.

Esther had no way of knowing that the king would hold out the golden sceptre and thus spare her life. (There is an element of uncertainty, humanly speaking, in every step of faith.) Nor did Esther know that Ahasuerus would accept her invitation to her banquet and eventually show mercy toward the Jews. The queen only knew she would do her best in that critical hour.

Had Esther acted in some frenzied manner then she probably would have failed in her mission. But Esther had fasted and prayed, and her manner was more of quiet confidence than of frenzy or fear. On the second day of the banquet which she had prepared for Ahasuerus and Haman, the queen revealed her cause. Her petition for the Jews was granted, and it was Haman who panicked. The king became enraged at his courtier's behavior. Haman was soon hanged on his own gallows.

In these difficult times, we too need the wisdom of the Almighty. We need to entertain our heavenly King and fellowship Him. The Lord Jesus should be invited to banquet with us before we share the great petitions of our hearts.

How Far Will I Go?

Many young people will go part way with their Savior. Under the influence of anointed preaching they may have gone to an altar and prayed. Again, feeling their need of being identified with Christ, they may have been baptized in the name of Jesus. Still others go farther and yield their lives to the baptism of the Holy Ghost.

The question, however, is not simply, "Will I go with Jesus?"; rather we need to ask ourselves, "How far will I go?"

Peter boasted that, "Though all men shall be offended because of thee, yet will I never be offended" (Matthew 26:33). From there he proceeded to Gethsemane where he fell asleep and acted in a very undisciplined manner. Next Peter was seen following the Lord "afar off unto the high priest's palace" (Matthew 26:58). While sitting with the servants in the palace and later when he moved out into the porch, Peter denied Jesus three times.

The depth of our commitment will likely be sorely tested in these last days. Today materialism and hedonism seem to prevail. The general attitude of many is to ignore, if not scorn, the church. Open antagonism towards Christianity may increase, especially as Christians take their stand on moral issues.

Like Paul, we must be determined to magnify Christ in our bodies, whether by life or death. (See Philippians 1:20-21.)

This world must know that we will go to any extent, face any danger, to serve our Lord. He, after all, is the One to whom all the glory belongs. Nothing else really matters.

Test Your Knowledge

1. What do we mean by the word *expendable?*
2. How many times is the name of God directly mentioned in the Book of Esther?
3. Why was Vashti deposed from being queen of Persia?
4. What was Haman's position in the kingdom?
5. What cunning plan did Haman propose to King Ahasuerus?
6. Who was Mordecai?
7. What characteristics did Mordecai display in the Book of Esther?
8. Why would Esther find Mordecai's command in chapter four frightening?
9. In what ways is our present day similar to Esther's situation in Persia?
10. What preparations did Esther make to gain her petition?

Apply Your Knowledge

Our God is not out to destroy us but to prove us. He sees the larger picture and the potential for good which lies behind every difficulty. The fact that He sees something worth developing in our character should be encouraging.

Consider the fact that the Lord has invested a great deal in you as a Christian. Are you committed to Him to the point of death, if need be?

Expand Your Knowledge

In the next chapter of this book you will read of some people in the Bible who were dependable and some who were not. Make a mental list of those whom you feel would fit each category. How would you account for the difference in the two groups?

11 Youth and Dependability

Moreover it is required in stewards, that a man be found faithful.

I Corinthians 4:2

Start With the Scriptures

Ruth 1
Proverbs 20:6
I Corinthians 6:1-8; 19-20
Matthew 25:14-30
Luke 16:1-12; 17:7-10

What is God like? How would we feel about God if He forgot to make the sun rise tomorrow? Suppose we were driving down a slippery two-lane road and suddenly our car careened out of control. We cry out, "Jesus, help me," but there is no response. Later, the Lord comes to us apologetically to explain that He simply forgot to come to work.

These ideas are absurd, but they make a point about the nature of God. God is dependable; we can always count on Him. Jeremiah commended the

Lord by saying, "Great is thy faithfulness" (Lamentations 3:23). Faithfulness is a biblical word that, in many cases, is a synonym for dependability.

Dependability Defined

Dependability is fulfilling what we agree to do even though it requires unexpected sacrifice. To be dependable a person must "be there, be on time, and be prepared."

As part of a fund-raising drive, a church youth group sponsored a car wash. Assignments were given to each youth committee member. One of the guys, Rick, was to make a large CAR WASH sign. At 9:00 A.M. the Saturday of the big event, a group showed up with buckets, sponges, and other car wash necessities, but there was no Rick, no sign, and no dirty cars. About an hour later, Rick showed up with a blank piece of poster paper and a felt-tip marker.

That was not an example of dependability. No doubt there were "reasons" for Rick's failure to come through on his agreement. However, reasons did not redeem the lost hour, or his lost credibility with the youth group. Rick was given the same job at the next car wash and came through with flying colors. Today, he is a successful professional in the church. Dependability was developed in his young life. We cannot succeed without it!

Stewardship and Dependability

In talking about any character quality, we must look at the "why" behind it. Why should we be dependable? What is the big deal about faithfulness? Spiritually and practically, it boils down to being accountable. All of us have to answer to someone. Ultimately, that someone is God. It also means that we answer to people who have authority over us. This whole idea can be expressed in a biblical word called stewardship.

A steward is someone who has been given charge of another person's property. "Or do you not know that your body is the temple of the Holy Spirit who is in you, whom you have from God, and you are not your own? For you were bought with a price: therefore glorify God in your body and in your spirit, which are God's" (I Corinthians 6:19-20, *NKJV*). We belong to God. Our time, our talents, and our treasures are really His. We are not free to live according to our own wishes. We are free from sin to serve Jesus Christ.

Stewards Must Be Dependable

"Moreover it is required in stewards, that a man be found faithful" (I Corinthians 4:2). Paul used the word *required* when writing of stewardship. In a society that urges self-expression and independence, this verse reminds us that God has a better way. For those who would boast, "I did it my way," Paul reminded us that faithfulness to God is non-negotiable. Dependability is a requirement. To say we are simply inconsistent or forgetful will not nullify the demand God makes.

A second powerful word Paul used is *found*. We are required to be "found" faithful. The idea that we are going to be found indicates that someone is looking. God is looking; He is looking for dependability. There will be a day of reckoning when God will examine all of His stewards. He will require that they all be found faithful. Stewards must be dependable.

The Parable of the Talents

The parable of the talents in Matthew 25 is an illustration of life and of our accountability to God.

Several features of this parable attract our attention.

- All of these people were servants who were made stewards. They were placed in charge of their master's money.
- All of them had something with which to work. Although their abilities were not equal, they all have some measure of potential. All of them were given talents—to one man five, to another two, and to the final man, one.
- Each man had the potential for individual success. To whom much was given, much was required. The one-talent man may have wished for five, but less was expected of him. He could be successful without competing against the other two. The master did not pit one against the other. They were competing only against their own potential.
- Not one of them was burdened beyond his ability. The wise master knew how much to put on them.
- All of them had to give an account. No one was exempt from answering for his actions. Upon the master's return and judgment upon the unprofitable servant, he said, "you knew...." It was no surprise that an accounting day was coming. Yet the one-talent man was not dependable with his talent.
- The master demanded dependability. The punishment of the unprofitable servant was outer darkness—a place of weeping and gnashing of teeth.
- Attitude made the difference. The servants' attitude toward their master and their talent determined what they did with what they had been given.

The statements of the profitable servants in contrast to those of the unprofitable man are interesting. The five-talent man said, "Lord, you delivered to me five talents; look, I have gained five more talents besides them" (Matthew 25:20, *NKJV*). He saw the talents as a gift from the master. The gift was an expression of the master's confidence in him as a servant. He saw himself in a partnership with his master. They were on the same team. He invited the master's scrutiny by saying "look," or as the King James Version states "behold." The profitable servant knew the master believed in him and would share in the excitement of his success. A right concept of the Master is a beginning point for dependable behavior.

Now let us consider the attitude of the unprofitable servant. Instead of viewing the talent as a gift, he saw it as a snare. His concept of the master was focused on the side of judgment. He saw the master as a hard, demanding enemy, looking for an opportunity to destroy him. The unprofitable servant did know the talent's origin and that he would be expected to return it. He handed the talent over in humiliation, not with a "behold," but saying, "lo, there thou hast that is thine." With all of the servant's excuses, the master cut through to the heart of the problem; "thou wicked and slothful servant." The unprofitable servant was lazy and his heart was not right.

What is our view of God? Do we see the abilities God has given us as a gift or a snare? Do we see God as our partner or our enemy? Our attitude toward ourselves and our God can make all the difference in our dependability.

Dependable in Least and in Much

Dependability is a character trait. If a person is dependable in small things, he will be dependable in large things, as well. "He that is faithful in that which is least is faithful also in much: and he that is unjust in the least is unjust also in much. If therefore ye have not been faithful in the unrighteous mammon, who will commit to your trust the true riches? And if ye have not been faithful in that which is another man's, who shall give you that which is your own?" (Luke 16:10-12).

It is to our advantage to be dependable in every area of our lives. God and men as well do not look at the size of the task, but our dependability to it.

Biblical "What If's?"

What if Ruth had gone back to Moab instead of cleaving to Naomi? Because her commitment to Naomi was a dependable one, she found a spot in the Bible—the ancestry of King David, and ultimately, the Messiah.

What if Joseph had given in to Potiphar's wife? The entire nation of Israel depended on Joseph's integrity. One man's dependable character saved a nation during a famine.

What if Esther had succumbed to the fear of rejection by King Ahasuerus? A nation hung in the balance, and who would have guessed that Esther had come to the kingdom for such a time as that? Esther was dependable to the point of risking her life for the sake of her people.

We cannot always assume that things will turn out right. There have been times when God sought for a man to make up the hedge and stand in the gap, and there was none (Ezekiel 22:30). We cannot leave life up to chance. God is depending on us.

Dependability Distractions

Dependability should be a normal trait easily found among ordinary people. Unfortunately, many people never learn the value and necessity of dependability. In our world, dependability is viewed as excellence, when actually it is the expectation of the average. Dependable people are rare. "Most men will proclaim every one his own goodness: but a faithful man who can find?" (Proverbs 20:6).

There are some things that distract us from being dependable. These must be overcome if we are to be found faithful.

Selfishness. Selfish people are usually inconsiderate. If their liberty inconveniences another, it is just too bad. After all, we could not expect them to go out of their way. If a selfish person decides that it is too much trouble to drive in the rain to help clean the church sanctuary, he will stay home. "There is no use risking my life when they will have plenty of help without me." However, the Bible teaches us to look out not only for our own interests, but also for the interests of others (Philippians 2:4). Dependability grows out of selflessness. We must consider the agenda of others, as well as ourselves.

Moodiness. People who are emotionally motivated are undependable. When they feel well, they do well. When they feel bad, they do badly. Moody people go from mountain to valley and back again. When they are up, they perform well, and expect the entire world to do the same. When they are down, they are critical and excuse themselves from being dependable.

Moodiness is an enemy of dependability and must be conquered. We must be rationally motivated. We must perform our duties regardless of our feelings. The Apostle Paul found help in conquering his moodiness by facing the consequences of losing the moodiness battle. "But I keep under my body, and bring it into subjection: lest. . .when I have preached to others, I myself should be a castaway" (I Corinthians 9:27).

Laziness. Lazy people are easily distracted from duty. It is interesting that a lazy person will seldom admit being lazy. They always have an excuse. "The slothful man says, 'There is a lion in the road! A fierce lion is in the streets!' As a door turns on its hinges, so does the slothful turn on his bed. The slothful man buries his hand in the bowl; it wearies him to bring it back to his mouth. The sluggard is wiser in his own eyes than seven men who can answer sensibly" (Proverbs 26:13-16, *NKJV*). One of the best ways to conquer laziness is with hunger. When a person gets hungry enough, he will usually go to work. If laziness is his weakness, however, there is a less painful solution. He should make himself accountable to someone else who will be honest, direct, and firm with him. He can submit to that person's authority without making excuses!

Poor Planning and Procrastination. This common dependability distraction can be conquered with discipline and forethought. When we have an obligation, we should write it down and plan other things around it. We can also plan in advance, keeping priority commitments free. To be more punctual, we can learn to count backwards. We should decide what time we want to be at a given appointment and count backwards for travel time and dressing time, and we then should leave a buffer for the unexpected. Phone calls and other distractions can make us appear undependable if we have not allowed time for such interruptions.

The main thing in life is to keep the most important things most important. We do not need to be sidetracked and fail to fulfill our assignment in life. Poor planning and procrastination should not be allowed to hinder our dependability.

Lack of Purpose. Probably the greatest deterrent to dependability is a lack of purpose. When we do not make ourselves important to anything, we will be undependable. The lack of a worthy purpose will destroy our motivation. Whether we are in maintenance or management, we can make ourselves important to that job. We can live by the conviction that things will not go as well when we are missing. In the church, we need to find at least one Christian involvement and make ourselves important to that ministry.

One man told of a personal hero of his church. "He was the man who cleaned and locked up the church where I was raised. Although his position was lightly esteemed, he was as dependable as the pastor. He possessed an expression of determination and purpose in his job. As he humbly carried out his duties, he worked as if he were a soldier in battle. Later, we learned of nights he walked several miles home alone. He stayed around until the job was finished. On occasion, I see him and observe his bent, aging body. A sense of respect wells up inside of me. I want to salute him for his dependability to the church."

We are as important as we make ourselves to any given task. It is not a matter of position or honor—but service. We can make a contribution with our lives. We can be dependable.

Who Is Depending on Us?

God is depending on us. Our character, devotion to Him, and worship are important. We are His ambassadors to the world. We are His witnesses and the temples of the Holy Ghost on this earth.

Our families are depending on us. The reputation we build will affect our families. The family units of which we are a part will be blessed or cursed by our contributions. There are responsibilities for us to handle.

The church is depending on us. The church is likened to a body made up of members with particular functions. As a part of the body of Christ, we are to maintain communication with the head of the body, Jesus Christ, develop harmony and unity within the body, and fulfill our particular functions. The church is depending on us. We should each ask ourselves this question, "If every member in our church was as dependable as I, what would the church be like?"

The world is depending on us. Jesus said that we are the salt of the earth and the light of the world (Matthew 5:13-16). Salt creates thirst and has been used as a preservative. Salt may refer to our invisible, spiritual influence. This invisible aspect of Christianity affects the spiritual thirst of a person. The more we develop our spiritual nature, the more we will affect our world. Light may possibly refer to our spoken and outward testimony, including our lifestyle. The world is depending on us to let our light so shine before them that they may see our good works and glorify our Father which is in heaven (Matthew 5:16).

The world is depending on our witness. We have a world to influence for Jesus Christ. There are people we each know who may have no other contact with God. We are their personal missionaries. They are our personal mission field. We should be dependable witnesses because the world is counting on us.

Displaying Dependability

How can a person display dependability? He can realize he is important and that he exists for a reason. At home, church, school or place of employment he can fill needs. He should be punctual and look for ways to advance every cause in his life. He can always do his best and never be satisfied with barely getting by. His full attention should be given to the task at hand. A person can control daydreaming and other mental vacations he takes and be consistent in everything. It is better to be a consecrated "plodder" than to be fickle and inconsistent. Dependability cannot be displayed by a single act, no matter how noble or impressive. It is over the long term of life that dependability pays off.

Test Your Knowledge

1. Dependability is _____ what we _____ to do, even though it requires _____ sacrifice.

2. A steward is someone who has been given _____ over another person's _____.

3. Quote I Corinthians 4:2: "_____."

4. A person who is faithful in that which is _____ is faithful also in _____.

5. List the five dependability distractions given in this chapter:
    A. _____
    B. _____
    C. _____
    D. _____
    E. _____

6. What we procrastinate we usually _____.

7. What are the three requirements of a member in the body of Christ?
    A. _____
    B. _____
    C. _____

8. In the parable of the talents, the three stewards were competing against their own _____.

9. The profitable servants in the parable of the talents saw the talents they received as a _____ while the unprofitable servant saw his

talent as a _____.

10. The major difference between the profitable servants and unprofitable servant was their _____ toward their master.

Apply Your Knowledge

Are you a dependable person? Make a chart with the days of the week along the top of the page, moving from Sunday on the left to Saturday on the right. Next, list your areas of responsibility on the left hand margin moving from top to bottom. You will want to include: prayer, fasting, church attendance, work/school, and other responsibilities. For the next week, fill in the spaces with the answers to the following questions.
1. Was I there?
2. Was I on time?
3. Was I prepared?
4. Did I do my best?

Make yourself accountable to a trusted friend. Ask him to critique you on your dependability level.

Expand Your Knowledge

1. Look up all the verses of Scripture listed in a complete concordance on faithfulness. Is dependability the same as faithfulness?
2. Read the book: Dayton, Edward R. and Engstrom, Ted W., *Strategy for Living*. Regal Books, Glendale, CA 1976.
3. Conduct an informal survey among church, business and educational leaders. Ask them what qualities they consider as most important to success.

12 Youth and Cooperation

That their hearts might be comforted, being knit together in love, and unto all riches of the full assurance of understanding, to the acknowledgement of the mystery of God, and of the Father, and of Christ;

In whom are hid all the treasures of wisdom and knowledge.

Colossians 2:2-3

Start With the Scriptures

Exodus 17:8-16
Judges 20:11
I Samuel 14:6-7
II Kings 6:1-3
Nehemiah 2:16-17
Matthew 18:19
Mark 2:3

The story is told of four men: Everybody, Somebody, Anybody, and Nobody. There was an important job to be done, and it seems that Everybody was sure that Somebody would do it. Anybody could have done it, but Nobody did. Consequently, Somebody got angry because it was Everybody's job. Everybody thought Somebody would do it, but Nobody asked Anybody. It ended up that the job never got done, and Everybody blamed Somebody.

Sadly, the world is filled with people who are

waiting for somebody else to do whatever needs to be done. "Let George do it" is the attitude of many. But what about the church? And how about the local youth group? How willing are we to help carry our share of the load?

As we delve into the Scriptures, we will discover that where God's people banded together, each doing his part, there God commanded His blessings.

What Is Cooperation?

The noun *cooperation* means "a joint effort of operation; mutual assistance; teamwork." *Cooperate,* a verb, is defined as "to act or work together with another or others for a common purpose; to combine in producing an effect." Synonymous expressions include the following: "unite one's efforts," "stand shoulder to shoulder," "join one's fortunes with," "pool one's interests," "enlist under the banner of," "as one man," "hand in hand," and "all for one, one for all."

Although the words *cooperation* and *cooperate* are never used in the Bible, the principle is scriptural. It is the underlying factor in many of the mighty exploits wrought by God's people. Most often it is described with expressions of togetherness, unity, and oneness.

The Scourge of Self-Sufficiency

Chuck Swindoll in *Strengthening Your Grip* observed that our society is becoming increasingly preoccupied with selfish interests. He wrote, "No longer are we a share-and-share-alike people. . . .We wear headsets as we jog or do our lawns or walk to class or eat in cafeterias. . . .our world is fast adopting the unwritten regulation so often observed in elevators, 'Absolutely no eye contact, talking, smiling, or relating without written permission from the management.'" He goes on to say, "We pursue self-sufficient lifestyles that make sharing unnecessary . . . .Anonymity, cynicism, and indifference are fast replacing mutual support and genuine interest."

This lack of adequate interaction has taken its toll on society. It has been shown to be a significant factor in a wide variety of social ills from depression to disease. It has sent many of its victims to prisons and mental institutions. And it has led some to end their own lives.

Dr. Paul Lee Tan illustrated this fact well. He told of a visitor to a mental asylum who was surprised that one lone guard armed with only a stick was standing watch over one hundred inmates. The curious visitor queried, "Aren't you afraid that these crazy people will get their heads together and plan to attack you?"

"Nah," replied the guard, obviously unconcerned. "These people are here because of their inability to get their heads together and work with others cooperatively."

Cooperation: A Mandate

Self-sufficiency is not a biblical concept. Neither is "doing one's own thing." The Scriptures stress the interrelatedness of mankind and the need for positive interaction among believers. In fact, Jesus Himself prayed that we "all may be one" (John 17:21).

The Apostle Paul compared believers to the various parts of the human body. He reminded the Corinthians that no part of a healthy body says to another body part, "I don't need you." (See I Corinthians 12:21.) Likewise in the body of Christ, there are no completely independent members. We all need each other.

Chinese humor has it that the feet once said to the mouth, "You are the luckiest thing on earth. You are forever getting the best of me. Here I am, running around all day, wearing myself out. And all for the sake of your eating."

The mouth snapped back, "Don't accuse me. How would you like it if I stopped eating so that you could stop running around?"

In order for the body of Christ to function effectively, individual members must work together as a team. As someone so aptly stated, "There are no effective loners in the church." But together we can change the world!

And using another analogy, the Apostle Paul compared believers to a temple for the habitation of God. Referring to the Lord Jesus, Paul wrote, "In whom all the building fitly framed together groweth unto an holy temple in the Lord: In whom ye are also builded together for an habitation of God through the Spirit" (Ephesians 2:21-22).

A Model of Cooperation

While Nehemiah was serving as royal cupbearer to King Artaxerxes I, he received word of the desolation of Jerusalem. The walls of the city were torn down, leaving it vulnerable to attacking armies and wild beasts. As a loyal Jew, Nehemiah was deeply moved and wept before the Lord.

In prayer Nehemiah committed himself to organizing the rebuilding of the walls of his ancestral city. The Lord in turn moved on the heart of the king, and he not only granted Nehemiah a leave of absence, but gave him building materials and letters of safe passage as well. But Nehemiah realized that obtaining the king's permission was but the first of many obstacles he had to overcome.

So with letters in hand, Nehemiah set out for

Jerusalem, confident that the hand of God was upon him, but knowing that he could not do the job alone. A few days after he arrived, he met with city leaders and rehearsed his plan to them. Fortunately, the men of the city did not respond the way some would today. They did not say, "Humph, who does this stranger think he is?" or "If we are content to live this way, what is it to him?" Instead, they said, "Let us rise up and build. So they strengthened their hands for this good work" (Nehemiah 2:18).

To get the job done, Nehemiah needed not only the support of city leadership, but he had to have the cooperation of the people as well. And he got it. Nehemiah divided the work on the wall into forty-two sections and assigned each family a section nearest his home. Fathers and sons worked side by side in a show of unity and strength.

Work on the wall was organized much like an assembly line. Each individual had a part to do. While one half of the laborers worked, the other half stood guard. These groups rotated in twelve-hour shifts.

The task was not without its problems, however. Opposition arose—as it usually does whenever God's people begin to make headway. The enemies of God's people began to laugh and mock. Motives were questioned and threats were made. Some of the workers became discouraged by the scope of the task and fear gripped many hearts when they heard the enemy's threats.

Nevertheless, the people worked on. Every worker labored with a sword at his side. And ever alert to danger, they ate standing up and never removed their clothes except to bathe. Thus the people toiled "from the rising of the morning till the stars appeared" (Nehemiah 4:21). And despite discouragement and opposition, the wall was completed in fifty-two days—a miracle!

What was the secret of this successful venture? Nehemiah stated it succinctly, "So built we the wall; and all the wall was joined together unto the half thereof: for the people had a mind to work" (Nehemiah 4:6).

Areas of Cooperation

Cooperation with God. Above all else, we must learn to cooperate with God. Refusing to do so often brings disastrous results. Willful King Saul lost his kingdom and eventually his life because he wanted to "do it his way" (I Samuel 15).

"Just what does cooperation with God entail?" one might wonder. First of all, we should consult Him before we make any plans. James wrote, "For that ye ought to say, If the Lord will, we shall live, and do this, or that" (James 4:15).

Secondly, we should surrender to God's will for our lives. Cooperating with God is not telling Him what we will do for Him, but rather resigning ourselves to Him and letting Him tell us what He wants to do with us.

Thirdly, we should throw ourselves wholeheartedly into the work of the Lord. After all, "we are labourers together with God" (I Corinthians 3:9). In fact, whatever our hands find to do, we should do it with all our might (Ecclesiastes 9:10).

And lastly, we must obey. As children of the Heavenly Father, we cooperate when we submit to His authority. The prophet Samuel reminded King Saul that "to obey is better than sacrifice" (I Samuel 15:22). And Jesus said, "If ye love me, keep my commandments" (John 14:15).

Cooperation with family. While harmony in the home should be the Christian norm, some teens cause turmoil by resisting the restrictions to their freedom that parents sometimes impose. There are those who deliberately ignore parental requests concerning curfews, dating, and doing household chores. Others resort to arguing, pouting, and angry words. God intended it to be otherwise.

The first step in maintaining family harmony is simply to honor one's parents. In fact, honoring one's parents is the first commandment with promise—a good and long life (Ephesians 6:2-3). Secondly, as long as it does not violate Christian principles, teens must obey their parents (Ephesians 6:1). Doing what we are told does not always please the flesh, but it is the will of God.

And where there are siblings, getting along is a must. Child experts say that siblings who do not interact positively grow up with psychological scars that last a lifetime. It is mentally and spiritually healthy to cooperate with one's brothers and sisters!

What is the solution to sibling rivalry? Preferring one another is essential. Possessing a good sense of humor, much tolerance and the willingness to share, and minimizing irritations and offenses helps. And lots of love goes a long way toward making the home a little bit of heaven on earth!

Cooperation with the church. Historians say that when the Roman army faced strong resistance, the soldiers positioned themselves shoulder to shoulder with their massive shields in front of them. Thus, like a moving wall, sometimes almost thirty miles long, the army advanced toward the enemy. When the enemy had wasted its arrows, the Romans moved in to conquer.

The church is constantly engaged in warfare with the forces of sin and Satan. To make strides against its foes, it needs people who are willing to unify their efforts. Moses reminded the Israelites that with the help of the Lord, one can chase a thousand and two can put ten thousand to flight (Deuteronomy 32:30).

Oh, the power of a united church! When we pray,

give, and work collectively, our efforts are intensified. For example, alone one person probably could not support even one missionary, but together we can send scores of missionary families around the world.

Cooperation with others. Aesop told the story of four bulls who were close friends and a lion who was eager to make them his dinner. The lion knew that he could take on any one of them alone, but not all four at once. So he devised a plan. When he noticed that one lagged behind the others, he would slip up and whisper that the other three had been saying unkind things about him. The scheming lion did this so often that the four bulls became uncomfortable in each other's company, each thinking that the others were conniving against him. Finally, with all trust destroyed, the bulls went off by themselves. This is what the lion wanted. He attacked them one by one and enjoyed four delicious dinners.

Satan operates much like Aesop's conniving lion. He seeks to separate us from fellow Christians, whom we need, and then moves in for the kill. The Apostle Peter warned, "Be sober, be vigilant; because your adversary the devil, as a roaring lion, walketh about, seeking whom he may devour" (I Peter 5:8).

It is God's desire that His children get along with all people as much as it is possible (Romans 12:18). The Apostle Paul offered this advice, "Live in harmony with one another; do not be haughty (snobbish, high-minded, exclusive), but readily adjust yourself to [people, things] and give yourselves to humble tasks. Never overestimate yourself or be wise in your own conceits" (Romans 12:16, *The Amplified Bible*).

Hindrances to Cooperation

Laziness. Some folks do not cooperate simply because they are plain lazy! Solomon advised, "Go to the ant, thou sluggard; consider her ways, and be wise" (Proverbs 6:6).

Mackay of Uganda, a denominational missionary, told how one day he saw a colony of soldier ants join their bodies together from the ground up to a tree branch. Up this living ladder the weaker ants climbed to a piece of meat which was suspended from a branch. Thus, even the frailest members of the ant colony had their needs supplied.

Fear. Fear paralyzes. It accents the dangers and hardships of any task. It can make obstacles seem insurmountable. But Paul assured us that we can do all things through Christ who strengthens us (Philippians 4:13).

Apathy. In order to get a job done, someone needs to say, "Let's do it! And then others must rise to the challenge. Had Nehemiah or the people been unconcerned, the wall never would have been built.

Jealousy. Sometimes jealousy provokes people to refuse to cooperate with a particular program or person. By refusing to lend their support, such folks hope the project will fail. When we sabotage another's progress, however, we ultimately hurt ourselves most.

Self-centeredness. There are times when in the interest of others, we must push aside our own desires and plans. For example, we might need to scrap plans for a shopping or fishing trip when the youth leader needs our help at a fund-raising car wash. We should remember the Apostle Paul's advice, "Let each of you esteem and look upon and be concerned for not [merely] his own interests, but also each for the interests of others (Philippians 2:4, *The Amplified Bible*).

Pride. Like Diotrephes, some people's egos prevent them from cooperating. (See III John 9-10.) They would be glad to get involved if it meant being in the limelight or receiving ample credit. But if they were in charge, they would, of course, expect—perhaps even demand—one hundred percent cooperation.

The Blessings of Cooperation

It refreshes and enriches. Psalm 133 contains one of the most poetic and beautiful descriptions of unity—or cooperation—in the Bible. The psalmist David declared, "Behold, how good and how pleasant it is for brethren to dwell together in unity! It is...as the dew of Hermon, and as the dew that descended upon the mountains of Zion: for there the LORD commanded the blessing, even life for evermore" (Psalm 133:1, 3).

It sustains in times of weakness. God had promised victory over the Amalekites to the children of Israel, but it was contingent on how Moses held his arms during the battle. When he held his arms up, Israel prevailed, and when he let them down, Amalek prevailed. Thus Aaron and Hur devised a plan. Each man stood on either side of Moses and held up his arms until Israel discomfited its enemy.

Alone, Moses would have succumbed to human weakness. With the support of Aaron and Hur, he was able to endure to victory. In like manner, there are people who need us to undergird them in their weak hour. If we accept the challenge, together we will share the sweet taste of victory.

It gives success in battle. Because of a great evil committed by the men of Gibeah, all the men of Israel "gathered against the city, knit together as one man" (Judges 20:11). As a united force, they were able to destroy the evil out of their midst. If we will stand fast in one spirit, with one mind striving together for the faith of the gospel, we too can win spiritual victories (Philippians 1:27).

It gives added power to prayer. Jesus Himself gave us a wonderful promise. He said, "Again I say unto you, That if two of you shall agree on earth as touching any thing that they shall ask, it shall be done for them of my Father which is in heaven" (Matthew 18:19). Great things can happen when young people unite in prayer! Unsaved family members can be won to God, sicknesses can be healed, and the fires of revival can spread throughout the congregation.

It brings a special presence of God. Jesus promised, "For where two or three are gathered together in my name, there am I in the midst of them" (Matthew 18:20). When we gather together in one accord, the Spirit of God is free to move unhindered among us. (See Acts 2:1-4.)

It helps bring men to Christ. Mark 2:3-12 records the incident of four men who brought a friend sick of the palsy to Jesus. Jesus honored their bold faith and healed the sick man and forgave his sins. Without the help and courage of his friends, the man never would have gotten near Jesus.

No one is interested in joining up with a group where discord is the prevailing condition. On the other hand, a spirit of loving cooperation attracts others like a sweet smelling fragrance. Each of us then should ask himself, "Am I helping to attract others or repel them from the Lord Jesus Christ and His church?"

Test Your Knowledge

1. What does *cooperation* mean?
2. List several synonymous expressions for the word *cooperate*.

3. What kinds of problems has lack of interaction caused in our society?

4. To what two things did the Apostle Paul compare the believers? What was the point he tried to get across?

5. Why was the building of the walls of Jerusalem a successful venture? List several reasons.

6. List four major areas of cooperation.

7. What are some hindrances to cooperation?

8. List as many blessings of cooperation as you can think of.

Apply Your Knowledge

For each of the four areas of cooperation discussed in this chapter, jot down several ways in which you can better cooperate.

Ask the Lord to help you follow through on your commitments to be a more cooperative person.

Expand Your Knowledge

If it were not for a group of auto workers on an assembly line, each doing his part, how many cars would we see on our roads? If it were not for a team of engineers and construction workers, how many bridges would span our waterways? If it were not for a team of dedicated anesthesiologists, doctors, and nurses, how many people would survive the operating room?

Continue this line of thinking and discover how empty our lives would be if everyone refused to work cooperatively with others.

You might find a book in the public library that shows how men have been able to accomplish great things through the power of cooperation.

13 Youth and Individuality

The Lord knoweth how to deliver the godly out of temptations, and to reserve the unjust unto the day of judgment to be punished.

II Peter 2:9

Start With the Scriptures

John 21:18-23
I Corinthians 12
Philemon 24
Colossians 4:14
II Timothy 4:1-11

Individuality is a word difficult to define. One might quickly think of it as "independence," but one can express his individuality without being an independent person.

Someone else might say that individuality is "doing one's own thing." In that sense they might be nearer the true definition as long as "doing one's own thing" is not an expression of rebellion, or refusing to do what is asked or required.

In his introduction to the first Corinthian letter,

Paul portrayed a bit of individuality. "Paul, called to be an apostle," he began in I Corinthians 1:1, introducing himself; then he addressed his audience by saying they are "called to be saints" (verse 2). The distinction between him (called to be an apostle) and them (called to be saints) is obvious.

Yet there is no boasting in Paul. He is not gloating with a sense of "big I, little you." He is simply stating, in a matter-of-fact way, that he has one calling from God and they have another. And perhaps that is as good a portrayal of individuality as we can find. "You have your job, talent, calling, etc., and I have mine."

One Church But Many Individuals

Paul described the church as a body, and he asked a rather humorous question: "If the whole body were an eye, where were the hearing?" (I Corinthians 12:17). The imagination draws a wild picture of a body with no legs, no arms, no feet, no nose, no ears, no face—nothing but one big eyeball! It is a hilarious illustration that Paul used to point out the significance that the church is comprised of many members, and each of them unique. It is a picture of individuality.

Individuality and the Gifts

"Are all apostles? are all prophets? are all teachers? are all workers of miracles? Have all the gifts of healing? do all speak with tongues? do all interpret?" (I Corinthians 12:29-30). The obviously implied answer to these questions is "No!" Therefore, Paul asserted the importance of recognizing that all Christians are unique and that it is critical that each one discover and develop his particular gifts.

No person who is ever used of God in the realm

of the gifts of the Spirit should ever boast of it. That he was used at all simply indicates that he has discovered his usefulness, at least in one area. It in no way suggests that he is closer to God or holier than others are. It only means that he has found something he can do in the kingdom of God. He has learned how to yield himself in that area. And the person so used should be wise enough to know that there are other areas in which he is not so easily used of God.

Neither should anyone ever be jealous of another who is used of God in a special, spiritual way. He should recognize that the other person has merely found a place of involvement in the work of God.

One dear elderly lady approached her pastor with a heartfelt confession about her own worthlessness in the church. "Pastor," she cried, "I feel that I'm just not good for anything! I come to every service, but I can't sing, I can't play an instrument, I have never given a message in another tongue, I have never interpreted a message. I can't get any of my friends to come to church with me, though Lord knows I've tried. It's always someone else who blesses the church with their talent. I wonder how I'm going to face God at judgment when there is nothing I can do for Him here?"

The pastor replied wisely: "My dear saint! Every week I see your tithing envelope in the offering, and I have learned that I can depend on you to support the church when I can't depend on others. When I ask for volunteers to come clean the church building, I always know that you will be here. I always know that every service I'll see your smiling face. One of those girls who sings so well never prays in the altar with sinners, but I know that any time a soul is searching for God in our church's altar, you will be right beside the person encouraging him in prayer. And one of our very talented musicians has let me know with her hands on her hips that she'll never sit in the nursery, while you have informed me often that if there's anything you can do, just call. I think you are very talented. I think you've found your place. So quit comparing yourself to what others are doing, and just keep on doing what you do best. Our church would be sadly lacking if you were not in it, doing just what you're doing."

Individuality in Avocation

Aside from the fact that God bestows different gifts and talents upon us, giving us complete individuality, He also arranges our lives so that we differ in vocation. The kingdom of God, therefore, lacks no quality, no skill, no job. And when a job is needed in some area, the kingdom lacks no man to send to fill that need.

The Corinthians did not understand this aspect of God-given vocation, and jealousies developed as members of the church formed little "fan clubs" for their spiritual mentors.

Paul was clear in his attempt to teach the Corinthians: "One saith, I am of Paul; and another, I am of Apollos; are ye not carnal? Who then is Paul, and who is Apollos, but ministers by whom ye believed, even as the Lord gave to every man? I have planted, Apollos watered; but God gave the increase" (I Corinthians 3:4-6). Paul had one job, and Apollos had another. God's call sent and equipped Paul to do one thing. God's call sent and equipped Apollos to do a different job altogether. The jobs that each of them performed in the kingdom of God were an expression of his individuality. There should be no cause for comparing and, subsequently, for jealousy. Each man is merely doing what God called him to do.

Other Examples of Individuality Expressed in Avocation

Luke was a physician. He could have stayed home and accumulated a clientele. He could have sought to earn himself a good living. But Luke obviously felt that God wanted him to travel with the Apostle Paul and to write. He did not seek to become a preacher himself. He did not attempt to become Paul's "agent." He apparently was content to occupy the role to which God called him. He did not have to try to be what others were.

Demas, on the other hand, had the privilege which many young ministers might have coveted. He was able to travel with Apostle Paul. However, he seemed not to appreciate the lot that had fallen to him. In his early ministry Paul referred to Demas as "my fellow labourer" (Philemon 24). Later Paul merely referred to him by name (Colossians 4:14). And finally, Paul wrote about him in a discouraging tone: Demas "hath forsaken me, having loved this present world" (II Timothy 4:10). That latter verse could be paraphrased to illustrate the point of this lesson: "Demas was not content in the role to which God had called him, and preferring to do something else, he forsook me."

Individuality, therefore, is not so much "doing your own thing," as it is "doing the thing to which God has called you."

Individuality and the Will of God

It is imperative, then, that a person know what God's will is concerning him since individuality rests upon his knowing and performing God's will.

The common call of God. Paul spoke of the Corinthians as being "called to be saints," but it is a description which fits the entire church, not just the

Corinthians. Hence, it is the will of God for every Christian to also be a saint. Without a lengthy exegesis, let it suffice to say that a saint is someone who is holy, or sanctified.

The will of God for any individual begins with total surrender to God. Romans 12:1-2 instructs us to present our bodies a "living sacrifice, holy, acceptable unto God." It refers to this act as a "reasonable service." It further admonishes us not to be "conformed to this world." And it concludes with "that ye may prove what is that good, and acceptable, and perfect, will of God."

The will of God allows much room for individual exercise and freedom of choice.

One man called it "God's Great Whatsoever." It is found in Ephesians 6:6-8: ". . .as the servants of Christ, doing the will of God from the heart; With good will doing service, as to the Lord, and not to men: Knowing that whatsoever good thing any man doeth, the same shall he receive of the Lord." Some men wrestle long over each particular action, worrying and sweating, hoping they are doing the perfect will of God, but this verse shows us that God has given a great "whatsoever!"

Each individual has been given lots of room to do different things, and as long as they are good things, they are within the will of God for us. Therefore, some do good things one way, some another, but each man is given room for his individual expression and service.

Moral purity is always God's will. In I Thessalonians 4:3, Paul wrote, "This is the will of God, even your sanctification, that ye should abstain from fornication." Some liberal modernists would have us believe that moral codes are changing, and the church should change its posture. They would convince us that each individual has a right to decide for himself if sexual relations outside the confines of marriage is for him or not. That is spiritual deception. Having individuality in no way means that one has liberty to sin. And immorality is and always has been sin. It is the will of God for every man and woman, regardless of his or her individual talents and gifts, to maintain a posture of sanctification and purity.

God's will involves our interpersonal relationships. No man is an island, and no man can say that he is doing the will of God "in his own way," if his own way means that he never gets involved with others. Some believe that they do not need to go to a church, that their individual walk with God somehow supersedes the need for church. But God's will requires involvement with others regardless of one's special talent or calling.

I Thessalonians 5:18 is often used as a text within itself, when it is actually the conclusion of a text. To find the beginning one must go to verse 11 which begins, "Wherefore...." Everything between "wherefore" and "for this is the will of God concerning you" (verse 18) should be read with the understanding that it is all the will of God concerning us. Therefore, the following list sums up God's will for all concerning brotherly relations:

- "Edify one another" (verse 11).
- "Esteem God's labourers very highly" (verses 12-13).
- "Warn the unruly" (verse 14).
- "Comfort the feebleminded" (verse 14).
- "Support the weak" (verse 14).
- "Be patient toward all men" (verse 14).
- "Do not render evil for evil" (verse 15).
- "Rejoice" (verse 16).
- "Pray without ceasing" (verse 17).
- "In every thing give thanks" (verse 18).

"For this is the will of God concerning you!" And let no man say that his individual gift or calling exempts him from such service.

What Individuality Means

Individuality means discovering that we are singularly different from all others. We are unique persons, designed by God, and equipped especially for some role in the local church in the kingdom of God. Of course, some are called to a labor beyond the local church, such as missionary work, evangelism ministries, and so on. But for the average individual, our talents and skills will be usable within the framework of our local church assembly.

Individuality also means discovering how we are different from others. In other words, it is not sufficient to just accept the fact that God made us especially for some task. We must know what that task is. It may be something very visible, like singing, or teaching classes. Or it may be like the lady mentioned earlier who thought she did very little, yet was a tremendous blessing to her pastor and played a significant role in bringing others to Christ.

Our difference, our individuality, does not make us "better" than others, nor does it make us "worse." It is simply that we have a different character, a different personality, a different talent, and a different function in the kingdom of God. Better or worse does not even enter the picture.

Individuality also means accepting others as they are. If we can accept that we have been wonderfully made by God and specially fitted for some task, then we can accept that every other person in our church has also been specially fitted for some task. If they are not like us, so be it. They should not be judged as being wrong, or stupid, or foolish just because they do not seem to see things the same way we see them.

Going to a brother whom we see at fault and attempting to correct him is not the same as criticizing everyone who does not see things our way. Others have their talents. Others have their viewpoints. Others are made by the same God who made us. We can accept their individuality and learn from them. We can marvel at how God has made us all so different, and yet the church of God seems to profit some from each different talent within it.

Individuality includes accepting ourselves as we are. Often we feel the need to make drastic changes in ourselves, not because the Holy Ghost has convicted us of some wrong, but rather because we have been in the presence of someone else whose talents and skills made us seem pale in comparison. We cannot be what others are, and should not even try to be. We are specially fitted for some place in the kingdom. We should find it and fit in.

One pastor had a young boy in his church who acquired the nickname "Xerox." Other youths teased the boy whom they had so nicknamed until the pastor felt sorry for him, and somewhat disappointed in them. Yet he found himself amused at the reason the nickname had been stuck on him in the first place.

It seemed that the young boy aspired to the ministry. Because of that aspiration, he loved to testify. Most often, his testimonies would sound very much like the pastor's most recent sermon, and most folks would smile and give a knowing wink to one another. But anytime a guest speaker would fill the pulpit, the boy's testimonies in church or Sunday school class would change tone and would resemble the guest's most recent sermon, right down to the mannerisms and an affected tone of the speaker.

Anyone who made an impression on the youth was copied precisely the very next time he got the chance to testify publicly. So the nickname was impossible to refute. However, the pastor recognized the dangerous symptoms of a boy who was not discovering his own personality and talent. In fact, he could not even find his own tone of voice. The pastor had to attempt some counseling to correct the problem.

While it may not be as obvious in most people as it was in that young boy, there is a tendency in all of us to emulate those who impress us strongly. There is a sense in which that is healthy, for we all need to be continually aiming for higher goals of self-improvement. But there is another sense in which such symptoms may reflect a general dissatisfaction with the way God has made us, and such a feeling needs to be corrected. Individuality is accepting ourselves as God has made us.

Individuality and Salvation

There is another aspect of individuality, and that is regarding salvation. No one will ever be saved because of the church he attends. No one will be saved just because he belongs to a Christian family. Obviously, attendance at a strong, Bible-teaching church, and birth into a Christian family are tremendously helpful regarding one's salvation. But in and of themselves, they represent no saving quality. Salvation is acquired strictly on an individual basis.

Every man is accountable personally to God for his own soul. The prayers of parents and friends may have tremendous power in getting God's attention, but they cannot save another. If we are to be saved, it will be because we (1) saw *ourselves* as sinners; (2) repented of *our* sins; (3) asked God to fill *us* with His Spirit; (4) and lived an obedient, holy life.

Salvation is an individual act!

Test Your Knowledge

True or False

_____ 1. One can express his individuality without being an independent person.
_____ 2. The church, as a body, is made up of many members.
_____ 3. Individuality is not so much "doing your own thing," as it is "doing the thing to which God has called you."
_____ 4. Individuality means discovering that we are singularly different from all others.
_____ 5. Individuality means discovering how we are different from others.
_____ 6. Our difference, our individuality, does not make us "better" than others.
_____ 7. Individuality means accepting others as they are, and ourselves as we are.
_____ 8. Salvation is acquired strictly on an individual basis.

Apply Your Knowledge

Review the meanings of individuality that are given in the chapter. As you review them, give thought to your own individuality. An honest look inward will help your personal growth in this area.

Expand Your Knowledge

Read biographies and autobiographies about great people. Notice their expressions of individuality and their lack of a "carbon-copy" mentality.
Look through the Bible, also. It contains many examples of such men and women.